CHURCH AND STATE

Smyth & Helwys Publishing, Inc.
6316 Peake Road
Macon, Georgia 31210-3960
1-800-747-3016

The paper used in this publication meets the minimum requirements of
American National Standard for Information Sciences—
Permanence of Paper for Printed Library Materials.
ANSI Z39.48–1984. (alk. paper)

ISBN-13: 978-0-9628455-4-3

CHURCH
AND
STATE

KARL BARTH

TRANSLATED BY G. RONALD HOWE

INTRODUCTION BY DAVID L. MUELLER

CONTENTS

INTRODUCTION

by David L. Mueller
Professor of Christian Theology
The Southern Baptist Theological Seminary

In an interview late in life, Barth commented: "Don't forget to say that I have always been interested in politics and consider that it belongs to the life of a theologian. My whole cellar is full of political literature. I read it all the time. I am also an ardent reader of the newspaper.[1] This remark recalls Barth's oft cited statement: "A Christian is one who reads both the Bible and newspaper. When one reads the newspaper, one should not forget what one has read in the Bible; and when one reads the Bible, one should not forget what one has read in the newspaper!"

These occasional statements are reflective of Barth's life-long engagement in politics evident both in his writings and political actions.

In spite of the overwhelming evidence pointing to the interrelationships between Barth's theology and his political stances and decisions, Hunsinger lists three recurrent objections to Barth's way of relating them.

One group of critics contends that Barth's theology is "inherently inadequate to the political realm" due to his excessive stress on God as "Wholly Other" and transcendent. Reinhold Niebuhr is representative in remarking that Barth views the political arena from "an eschatological airplane" making it impossible for him to provide guidance in the complexities of ethical and political decision making.[2]

A second group of objectors follows Charles West in maintaining that Barth's "political judgments" are made without reference to any serious "empirical analysis." This inattention to the "facts of human experience" stems from an excessive preoccupation with God's grace as the resolution to all ethical and political issues.[3]

Barth's third group of critics contends that the gap between his theology and politics is so great that he cannot relate them consistently. Thus he relates the two in "ad hoc, and finally arbitrary" ways. [4] This inconsistency is attributed either to his personal experiences with various political and social forces such as socialism, German National Socialism, democracy, capitalism, and communism or to his personal psychological make-up marked by a consistent desire to go "against the stream" of prevailing theological and political opinion. Emil Brunner, Reinhold Niebuhr, and others interpreted Barth's refusal to condemn totalitarian communism in the period following World War II in the same manner he had opposed Nazi totalitarianism in the thirties as indicative of his inconsistency. These critics concur that Barth is first and foremost concerned with theory and formal theology and not with concrete political and ethical issues.[5] Some even explain Barth's changing political stances in terms of the young liberal and radical becoming more conservative with age.

Hunsinger observes that if Barth's critics are correct, readers of Barth are confronted with a "genuine anomaly." He continues:

> One of the most fundamental Christian thinkers of modern times, with a deep personal interest in politics, proved conceptually incapable of integrating his political decisions with his formal thought. He could achieve no intrinsic relationship between them; his politics stayed fundamentally cut off from his theology. Barth the "politician" and Barth the theologian remain unreconciled in thought.[6]

Barth's Early Development (1886–1920)

It is not possible to pursue the current controversy regarding the relationship of Barth's theology to his politics exacerbated, particularly in Germany, through the publication of Friedrich-Wilhelm Marquardt's controversial book. He argues that Barth's decisive theological shift is attributable to the inner connections between his socialism and what Barth in his commentary on Romans referred to as "God's revolution."' Here it must suffice to point to some decisive events and developments in Barth's theology prior to the publication of "Church and State" in 1938.

Crucial in Barth's early development (1886–1904) was the influence of the Reformed or Calvinistic tradition in his family, Church, and environment. As the son of a Reformed minister and professor of Church History and New Testament exegesis, Barth's faith was nurtured both at home and in a Reformed tradition moderately conservative, scholarly, and socially sensitive. During his theological studies (1904–1909), Barth increasingly moved from his Reformed roots into the camp of theological liberalism dominating European theology. Upon his graduation and ordination (1909), he viewed himself as a somewhat tentative theological liberal. Prior to assuming a pastorate, he served on the editorial staff of the influential liberal periodical, *Die Christliche Welt*, which focused on the church's mission to usher in the kingdom of God through social action.

During his first few years in the pastorate (1909–1911) in Geneva and Safenwil, Switzerland, Barth tentatively espoused a form of liberal theology which stressed individual religious experience on the one hand and "historical relativism" with respect to Christian truth claims on the other. Confronted as a pastor with "the need and promise of Christian preaching," Barth said:

> I sought to find my way between the problem of human life on the one hand and the content of the Bible on the other. As a minister I wanted to speak to the *people* in the infinite contradiction of their life, but to speak the no less infinite message of the *Bible*, which was as much of a riddle as life.[8]

During his pastorate in Safenwil (1911–1921), a small industrial village, Barth worked hard on the preparation of sermons and on helping to develop the trade union movement along socialist lines. Encountering "class warfare" in his own parish and canton caused Barth to rethink his previous unquestioned identification of the advancement of the kingdom of God with capitalism. Soon after arriving in Safenwil, he spoke to the local labor union on "Jesus Christ and the Movement for Social Justice."' Indeed, Barth was so identified with socialism that he was referred to as the "Red Pastor" or as "Comrade Pastor." Beginning about 1914, Barth's view of society also was influenced through his acquaintance with the "kingdom of God" theology of the elder and younger Blumhardt. These pietistic Lutheran ministers interpreted the advance of God's kingdom in terms of Christ's continuing victory over the powers of darkness and evil. Their vision contributed to the movement of Swiss Religious Socialism which exerted considerable influence on Barth and others during this period. It saw God's will being realized through the rising socialist labor movement.

Some twenty years earlier, the young Baptist minister, Walter Rauschenbusch, also influenced by the theology of Ritschl and Religious/Christian socialism, anticipated Barth's Christian socialism in his struggle with the meaning of the gospel in his parish in Hell's Kitchen in New York City. Like Rauschenbusch, Barth's Christian socialism combined theory and practice. In this regard, he differed from his contemporary, Paul Tiffich, who was identified as a theoretician of religious socialism. In 1915, Barth felt impelled to join the Social-Democratic Party—

an unheard of action for a Swiss minister at that time. He
did so stating that

> it was no longer possible for me personally to remain
> suspended in the clouds above the present evil world
> but rather it had to be demonstrated here and now that
> faith in the Greatest does not exclude but rather
> includes within it work and suffering in the realm of
> the imperfect.[10]

Protestant liberalism lost even more of its luster for
Karl Barth in 1914 when ninety-three German intellectu-
als, including most of Barth's former theological mentors,
signed a manifesto endorsing the German Kaiser and the
German war policy. Barth commented then and later that
such an uncritical nationalism was indicative of a diseased
Christian ethic derived from a sick theology! Though
living in neutral Switzerland, the Great War raged through
Barth's soul and his sermons. One woman complained
that his sermons had far too many allusions to the war!
But it was not finally the war which changed Barth's mind,
but the "strange new world within the Bible." The exeget-
ical studies characteristic of this period came to flower in
Barth's commentary on Romans first published in 1919.
Barth's concentration on the crisis of Western history was
not precipitated primarily by the catastrophe of World
War I. Rather, for Barth, the war reflected humanity's sin-
fulness already so abundantly attested in the Bible. In both
editions of his Romans commentary (1919, 1922), Barth's
primary aim was not to thunder about God's judgment of
sinful humanity as the first and last word to be said. To be
sure, he opposed a liberal theology which preached a
gospel of human goodness necessitating no divine judg-

ment—no cross—and no need of repentance. He also rejected liberalism's identification of Western culture with the kingdom of God. But Barth saw quite clearly that the last word, which indeed is the first word, is the word of God's grace in Jesus Christ. He, Jesus Christ, is no ordinary human word unable to save, but the Word of God come from above, the "Wholly Other" One, who enters human history to effect a new creation. In his life and ministry, and supremely through his cross and resurrection from the dead by the power of God, the new world had dawned. Ultimately, it was the Apostle Paul's proclamation of this word of God's grace in Jesus Christ which Barth intended to echo in his commentar.[11]

Toward a Theology of the Word of God (1921–1938)

In the Preface to the second edition of his commentary on Romans (1922) written just before Barth's move to a professorship in Germany, he spoke of his theological ancestry. He traced it through Kierkegaard, Luther and Calvin and finally to Paul and Jeremiah. Increasingly, he saw Protestant liberalism as a defection both from the Reformers and the witness of the Bible.

Here it must suffice to identify some of the major Reformation emphases which left an indelible mark on Barth's developing theology during the decade from 1921–1931.

(1) Barth's total energies were dedicated to the attempt to establish theology on the Word of God attested in the Scriptures rather than on Christian piety or experience. He also rejected beginning with a purported immanence of God in human history, culture, or human consciousness

in the manner of natural theology. In short, Barth's intention was to point to the sovereign God through whose initiative alone God could be known.

(2) Over against the loss of a radical doctrine of human fallenness in Protestant liberalism, Barth reasserted humanity's alienation and lostness. Humanity was neither good nor getting better and without need of God's saving grace.

(3) Ever more surely, Barth's focus on God's revelatory activity in his words and acts attested in Scripture led him to develop a strongly christocentric theology reminiscent of the Reformers. This necessitated his polemic against liberalism's tendency to view God and revelation in terms of the human self rather than in the light of God revealed in Jesus Christ.

(4) Like the Reformers, Barth's theology focuses on God's sovereign grace. The message of *sola gratia* (grace alone) echoes throughout: his theology becomes a witness to the "triumph of grace" (G. C. Berkouwer).

(5) Barth's theology, like that of the Reformers, locates the center of God's saving grace in the suffering and death of Jesus Christ. In this way Barth reappropriates and develops a *theologia crucis* (theology of the cross) central in both Luther and Calvin.

(6) Barth's theology seeks to advance the Reformation heritage in its confession of the primary authority of Holy Scripture for determining the true nature of Christian faith, truth, practice, worship and theology. The emphasis on *sola Scriptura* (Scripture alone) is non-negotiable. In agreement with the Reformers, Barth regards the Confessions of the Church to have an authority subordinate to that of Holy Scripture. Like the Reformers, Barth

distinguishes inspired Scripture from the revelation it attests. However, he rejects Protestant Orthodoxy's view of biblical inerrancy as a rationalistic theory which cannot be supported on the basis of a serious study of what the Bible says about itself. It falls to take the humanity of the biblical witnesses seriously in addition to disregarding the facts of the Bible's origins and development.

(7) Barth's theology of grace like that of the Reformers reiterates their emphasis on justification through faith alone (*sola fide*). Every believer comes to faith through the Holy Spirit who vivifies both the written and preached Word. Faith is neither self-generated nor is it individual spiritual experience separable from Jesus Christ attested in Scripture.[12]

The German Church Struggle: The Road to Barmen (1932–1934)

In his masterful study of the German Church struggle, Arthur Cochrane traces the way in which the German Evangelical Church continued to support the German nationalistic and militaristic spirit after World War I. It was against labor and socialism as materialistic. Above all, it wanted to preserve its legal rights and privileges in relationship to the State. Many Church leaders supported Hitler's National Socialist Party. They founded Church organizations anticipating the establishment of the German Christian movement in 1933.[13] In an address on "The Desirability and Possibility of a Universal Reformed Creed" in 1925, Barth spoke prophetically of a theological and ethical flabbiness characteristic both of his own Reformed Church and others. He said:

> We see the Church of today in no sure position, waver-
> ing between yes and no, even more in ethics than in
> dogmatics; now silent where it ought to speak, now
> speaking where it ought to be silent; always...behind
> what the world has done without it;...full of goodwill
> towards all sides; but certainly, very certainly it raises
> no prophetic voice, no watchman's cry, above the con-
> fusion of other voices. Is it different...in America?
> Really different than in Germany and in Switzerland,
> of which again I think first?[14]

The German Christian movement was in place six
months before Hitler's accession to power in January,
1930. It united Protestants holding in common "nationalistic tendencies and liberal Christianity."[15] These German
Christians applauded Hitler's Party Platform enunciated
prior to his election; it declared that the Nazi Party took
"the standpoint of 'positive Christianity'" without being
"bound to any particular Confession of Faith." Hitler
guaranteed freedom to all Churches and religious groups
provided "they do not endanger the existence of the State
or do not offend the moral and ethical conscience of the
Germanic race."[16] The German Christian Platform left
theological affirmations aside in giving unqualified support to the major principles of the Nazi party, namely:
"positive Christianity; the fight against Marxism, the Jews,
internationalism, and Free Masonry; preservation of the
purity of the race; and defense of the people against degen-
eration."[17]

Welcoming the support of the German Christians,
Hitler intervened immediately into the affairs of the
Evangelical Church by appointing his crony as the ruling
Bishop. An overwhelming majority of Protestants, includ-

ing Baptists and others representing the Free churches, as well as the Roman Catholic Church, were enthusiastic in support of Hitler and National Socialism. Yet even before Hitler's election, a prophetic minority arose in the Protestant Church in opposition to the synthesis of the Christian faith and Nazism. Among its leading figures was Karl Barth. These Protestants regarded themselves as representatives of the true Evangelical Church of Germany; they became known as the "Confessing Church." For a few short months, Barth and others in the Confessing Church expressed opposition to the German Christians in the journal, *Theological Existence Today*, which Barth helped establish in July, 1933. Confronted with the increasing defection of theologians to the German Christians—including some like Gogarten associated with Barth and a co-editor of the journal—Barth wrote an angry editorial "Farewell" in what proved to be the journal's final issue. Pointedly, Barth attacked the German Christian heresy:

> I for my part always opposed precisely that which can now be seen in concentrated form in the doctrine, mentality and stance of the German Christians. I cannot see anything in them but the last, fullest and worst monstrosity of the essense of Neo-Protestantism [i.e., liberalism]....My *view is that our journal* could have been the voice of the true Church in our time only if it stood as a modest but unbreakable dam against the overwhelming tide of the German-Christian flood.[18]

In 1945, Barth lamented that the resistance of the Confessing Church to National Socialism "was not a total resistance against totalitarian National Socialism. It confined itself to the Church's Confession, to the Church service, and to Church order as such. It was only a partial resistance."[19] Yet Barth took solace in the fact that it did more than the universities, press, law, business, the arts, army, or trade unions which offered no resistance. Albert Einstein, the renowned Jewish physicist, corroborated Barth's estimate after being exiled from Germany by the Nazis. He also had looked to the above institutions to support the cause of truth and freedom of inquiry. They did not. He wrote:

> Only the Church [the Confessing Church] stood squarely across the path of Hitler's campaign for suppressing the truth. I never had any special interest in the Church before, but now I feel a great affection and admiration because the Church alone has had the courage and persistence to stand for intellectual and moral freedom. I am forced to confess that what I once despised I now praise unreservedly.[20]

On Hitler's accession to power, the German Christians dominated the Evangelical Church. With the support of the Nazi State, they used all available means of propaganda, intimidation, and the politicization of Church elections in order to take over the leadership and control of the Church and to crush the Confessing Church. Following World War I, the Evangelical Church had been disestablished, but along with other Churches continued to receive State support and retain ties to the State. Recognizing that the Confessing Church represented a threat to their complete political control of the Evangelical Church, the German Christians desired to be identified as "the" State Church of Germany.

In seeking Hitler's approval of their movement as representative of the State Church of the German nation, the German Christians adopted a Platform of "Guiding Principles" (1932) for the reorganization of the "German Evangelical Federation of Churches" into "one Evangelical State Church."" Among the strategies they employed to gain recognition as "the" State Church of the German Reich were the following: (1) unqualified support of Hitler and his totalitarian State; (2) rejection of "parliamentarianism [as outdated] even in the Church"" and acceptance by the Church of the "Führerprinzip," that is, of the principle of the "absolute leader," ruling the Church as its chief Bishop; and (3) unquestioning patriotism and the rejection of all pacifism and "internationalism" in politics; (4) acceptance of the superiority of the German race and nation; (5) support of all measures to maintain the "purity" of the Aryan race; (6) support both of the State's anti-Semitic program and opposition to undesirable minorities who are "unfit and inferior"; (7) the necessity to wage war against Marxism as anti-godly and as a threat to the State; (8) undermining the Bible's *authority by* subordinating its teachings to the Nazi ideology; (9) the politicization of Church government through the adoption of a system of appointments based on political allegiance rather than on spiritual qualifications; (10) the destruction of theological education through appointments based on political alignments rather than on competence; (11) the identification of the advance of the Nazi Reich and cause with the coming of the kingdom of God.

It was against this politicization of the gospel and the Church that the Confessing Church struggled in the two

years prior to the meeting of the Synod of Barmen, May
29–31, 1934. Barth was among the most prophetic voices
in the Confessing Church before Barmen. For this reason,
he and two Lutherans were appointed to provide an initial
draft of a "Confession of Faith" to be presented to the
Synod of the Confessing Church at Barmen. After their
initial deliberations, Barth notes that his two Lutheran
colleagues took a nap while the "Reformed Church kept
awake." Recalling the event some years later, Barth commented: "I revised the text of the six statements, fortified
by strong coffee and one or two Brazilian cigars. The result
was that by evening there was a text. I don't want to boast,
but it was really my text.[23]

Barth's views on the relationship of Church and State
were hammered out in the German Church struggle and
find their clearest expression in the Barmen Declaration.
This Declaration of the Confessing Church intends to be
faithful to the lordship of Jesus Christ attested in Holy
Scriptures and to the historic Lutheran and Reformed
Confessions of the Reformation. The Preamble depicts the
German Christian movement as a heresy destructive of the
unity of the Church due to its adoption of "false doctrine," the "use of force and insincere practices," and
illegitimate "teaching methods and actions." In Barmen's
First Article, the Church confesses that Jesus Christ "is the
one Word of God" who calls for trust and obedience "in
life and in death." It condemns the German Christian synthesis of Jesus Christ and Nazis, as twin sources of the
faith and witness of the Church. All similar syntheses are
also repudiated. In its unqualified christological focus, it
bears the unmistakable stamp of Barth's theology. At
Barmen, the Confessing Church condemned the German

Christian heresy as a pernicious example of natural theology which recognizes other sources of the true knowledge of God which by—passes God's definitive revelation in Jesus Christ. It does so by proclaiming in "race, folk, and nation, [as] orders of existence granted and entrusted to us by God," a second source of the knowledge of God alongside of Jesus Christ. [24] In the First Article, the Church confesses:

> Jesus Christ, as he is attested for us in Holy Scripture, is the one Word of God which we have to hear and which we have to trust and obey in life and in death. We reject the false doctrine, as though the Church could and would have to acknowledge as a source of its proclamation, apart from and besides this one Word of God, still other events and powers, figures and truths, as God's revelation. [25]

The Fourth Article calls for the exercise of the Church's ministry to be that of the servant in keeping with Jesus' life and admonition (Matt. 20:25-26). It warns against the "exercise of the ministry" in the form of "a dominion of some over the others," and calls for the ministry of the "whole congregation." It rejects as "false doctrine" the German Christian principle of the "absolute ruler" who either gains power in the Church or is given such by the State.

The Fifth Article deals with the relationship of Church and State. Here and in each Article the concrete political and ethical issues relevant to what is confessed are not sidestepped, but addressed. Thus while the "divine appointment" of the State and its calling to provide for "justice and peace" is gratefully acknowledged, Barmen

rejects the concept of the totalitarian State as a "false doctrine" permitting the State to transcend its divinely
appointed bounds by taking on the characteristics of the
Church. The German Christian Church is condemned as
heretical in transcending its commission by taking on the
character of the State, "and thus itself becoming an organ
of the State."[26] In Article Six, the Church's commission to
declare the Word of God in freedom and obedience is
affirmed in opposition to the German Christian heresy of
using the Church's proclamation to advance the political
ideology of right-wing Nazi Fascism.

Barmen marked a kairotic event in struggle of the
Confessing Church against the German Christian heresy
within the Church and an idolatrous State without. Barth
continued to play an important role in that conflict.
Increasingly, however, he became *persona non grata* in the
eyes of the Nazi State. He desisted from swearing uncondi-
tional allegiance to Hitler as required of every civil servant.
He refused to begin his lectures with the required greeting,
"*Heil Hitler!*" These offenses, coupled with his leadership
in the Confessing Church, led to his expulsion from
Germany to Switzerland in 1935. Shortly before his depar-
ture, he wrote his angry "No!" to Emil Brunner for
appearing to lend theological support to the natural theology of the German Christians in his article on "Nature
and Grace."

From neutral Switzerland, Barth continued his intense
theological and political activity in support of the
Confessional Church. Many of his writings and lectures in
the decade of the thirties reflect this conflict. His influential work on Anselm (1931) and the publication of the
first two volumes of the *Church Dogmatics* (I/1, I/2) show

how his theocentric and christocentric theology provided the foundation for his political judgments and actions.[27] Indeed, a collection of his writings dealing with the Church conflict in Germany and issues related to World War II (1938–1945) attest that Barth regarded his political activity and publications before, during, and after the war as part of his "political service of God." By virtue of his many communications to the allied nations, Churches, and Christians during the war, he became a leading international voice calling for the overthrow and defeat of Nazi Germany.[28]

Barth's lecture on *Church and State* was published in 1938. In order to understand the direction of Barth's thought, the reader would do well to read it in conjunction with another lecture delivered just six months later. It was entitled, *The Church and the Political Problem of Our Day* (1939). In the latter, Barth is more outspoken in his attack upon the German Christian heresy and the evils of the Nazi totalitarian State. This is due, in part, to the fact that in *Church and State*, Barth is building his case exegetically whereas the 1939 lecture is more popular in form. Barth's most thematic expansion of the same theme is found in his lecture, *The Christian Community and the Civil Community*, given in Germany shortly after the war's end and published in 1946.[29]

Church and State: Summary Theses

Barth's concern in *Church and State is* to ascertain whether there is a connection between God's justification of sinful humanity through Jesus Christ and human law and justice. This requires searching the New Testament to

determine whether there is a "vital connection" between
the Church's worship of God on the one hand and its
"political' service of God" related to issues of human law
and justice on the other.[30]

INTRODUCTION

1. While acknowledging that the Reformers rightly
recognized the divine ordination and respective responsibilities of both Church and State, Barth faults them for
failing to relate their confession of justification through
Christ and his lordship to their interpretations of the State
and the issues of human law and justice. Instead, the
Reformers viewed the State and its law either in terms of a
nebulous "divine providence" or in light of non-biblical
norms of justice.

2. This failure gave rise to two later misinterpretations.
First a pietistic and quietistic stance encouraged the separation of a pure Church from the State while confessing
God's lordship in all spheres. This precluded relating God's
lordship to issues of human justice. This perspective is
related to the Lutheran doctrine of the "two kingdoms,"
spiritual and civil, which encouraged Christians in Nazi
Germany to submit unquestioningly to the State's divinely
ordained authority. Second, the Enlightenment severed
human law from any reference to God's justice manifested
in Jesus Christ while often relating human law to a universal divine providence.

Barth proposes a more adequate biblical and christological view of their relationships adequate to "the
intensity of our present situation."

I. The Church and State as They Confront One Another

Barth faults the Reformers for interpreting Jesus' confrontation with Pilate solely in terms of the separation or opposition between God's kingdom, or the realm of redemption, and the State. He interprets their encounter as revelatory of their interrelatedness. Pilate "was the human created instrument of that justification of sinful man that was completed once for all time through that very crucifixion." Hence, Barth finds in the encounter between Jesus and Pilate that even the "demonic" State which wills evil "may be constrained [by God] to do good." In this manner, Pilate, as the representative of the State, "became the involuntary agent and herald of divine justification."

II. The Essence of the State

1. The State is ordained of God and invested with authority in order to govern justly. However, even a demonic State in the final analysis will be unable to thwart its original divine determination in and through the Son of God. Nor will the State be able to withstand the Son's eschatological vindication over it and all lesser powers. Since the State "belongs originally and ultimately to Jesus Christ,…it should serve…Jesus Christ and therefore the justification of the sinner."

2. A State becomes demonic not when it is "autonomous" and exercises a "relative independence" from the Church, but when its absolute claims entail a divinizing of the State. This is what occurred in the Nazi State.

3. Barth's attempt to view the State christologically represents his correction of the perspectives of the Reformers, the Nazi State, and the German Christians. They represent a larger tradition which interpreted the State and human law in terms of God, the Creator, or in terms of divine providence, without any reference to Jesus Christ.

4. The State fulfills its purpose in granting the Church freedom to proclaim "the gospel of justification" to all peoples—including the State. In so doing, the State is an indirect witness to God's grace in Jesus Christ. The Church must exercise constant vigilance regarding the State's actions in this regard.

III. The Significance of the State for the Church

1. The New Testament reckons with the contrast between Church and State because the Christian's ultimate citizenship is in heaven. Nevertheless, hope in Jesus Christ enables faith to discern to some degree the will of Christ accomplished in the State. The limited glory of the earthly State will one day contribute to the "political order" of the "real heavenly State," the "heavenly Jerusalem." This hope precludes either deifying the State or identifying it too hastily as a demonic State.

2. The New Testament contrast between the earthly and heavenly State was the consequence of faith's confidence that God's justification was the "true and only real source" of all human law. Hence the Church's preaching of justification provides the foundation of the State and its law.

3. Proclamation of God's accomplished justification through Jesus Christ as God's "Eternal law" countenances neither the Church's usurpation of the State's rightful role nor its identification of itself as the realized "heavenly State." Both Rome and "fanatical sects" succumbed to these errors.

It is lamentable that currently some Southern Baptists seem to have lost appreciation both for the historic Baptist position on the separation of Church and State and the First Amendment of the American Constitution. Barth's warning against "fanatical" sects desirous of establishing a clerical or theocratic State needs to be heeded. History provides ample testimony to the wisdom of this separation. Baptists who fought and died for a "free church in a free state" need to be zealous to preserve this principle of "religious liberty" in accordance with Article 17 of "The Baptist Faith and Message" (1963).

4. The New Testament distinction between Church and State does not do away with their reciprocal responsibilities. The State is responsible for granting the Church freedom to proclaim the Gospel; the Church acknowledges the divine ordination of the State and its rightful sphere of authority and jurisdiction. Prayers of intercession are to be offered by the Church in behalf of the State— even when it does not grant the Church freedom to proclaim the Gospel.

5. Barth maintains that when the New Testament views the State christologically, it is able to speak positively of the State. It is ordained to establish human justice and to grant the church freedom to proclaim God's universal saving will within its orbit. Viewed thus, the State is subordinate to God's ultimate lordship and indirectly

advances God's reconciliation of the world to himself accomplished in Jesus Christ.

IV. The Service of the State for the Church

1. The Church is enjoined to pray for the State in light of its divine ordination irrespective of whether it is a just or unjust State. In doing so, the Church reminds the State of its limits.

2. If the Church's freedom is restricted by an evil State, it serves the State through passive and active resistance rather than through obedience.

3. The Church "expects the best" of the State in light of its divine legitimation and subordination to the lordship of Jesus Christ.

4. The Christian's observance of the law of the State legitimates human law "from the standpoint of the divine justification" of sinners who always seek to justify themselves and "to escape from true law."

5. The Christian's necessary allegiance to the State precludes making an oath of absolute loyalty to a totalitarian State and its claims. Nazi requirements of its citizens in this regard signify the State's self deification. Therewith it becomes an unjust or demonic State.

6. Responsible Christian citizenship today entails prayer for the State, political action, and "political struggle." Such action is responsible for the rise of the democratic State.

7. In utilizing the freedom granted it to proclaim "divine justification," the Church serves the establishment and preservation of human law which avoids both tyranny and anarchy. 8. Although the just State serves the reign of

justice and peace and concern for human welfare, it is neither called nor able to usher in the kingdom of God.

9. Therefore, Barth seeks to avoid Protestant liberalism's tendency to equate the advance of Western capitalist civilization with the kingdom of God. As a liberal, Barth was sympathetic toward this view. As a Christian socialist, he tended to equate the socialist State with the coming kingdom. Further reflection on Scripture led Barth to become critical of all identifications of historical States and social systems with God's coming kingdom. Nevertheless, he insists that the just State marked by a reign of peace and justice may be an "image of Him whose Kingdom will be a Kingdom of Peace without frontiers and without end."

10. God's patience is given to the end that the Church's central proclamation of God's justification of sinful humanity might be heard and acknowledged by all in the State and the world. In this way, God's saving purpose for each person and the entire world will be realized on earth "in the midst of the great but temporary contrast between Church and State." When that occurs both Church and State will reflect here and now God's coming perfect kingdom wherein God's lordship transcending both Church and State will be revealed.

Postscript: A Baptist Reflection

What does Barth have to say to Southern Baptists regarding the relationship of Church and State? We must recall that Barth struggled throughout his life with the teaching of Scripture and his own Reformed tradition in the attempt to speak and act faithfully on the issues per-

taining to the right relationship between Church and
State. Our analysis of his position has been restricted in
the main to one of his many writings on this subject." At
all times and in changing situations he sought to speak
and act responsibly under the lordship of Jesus Christ.
Southern Baptists can do no less. Preserving our heritage
of a "free church in a free state" as affirmed in "The
Baptist Faith and Message" (Article 17) of 1963 requires
constant vigilance. At several points Barth's interpretation
of Scripture calls us to a serious reconsideration of our
own heritage relating to the separation of Church and
State.

What are some questions Barth would put to us as
Baptists in this regard? First, he might ask us whether we
are clear about our mission as a "free church" in our society? To what extent is our profession of the lordship of
Jesus Christ lived out in our churches, in our lives and in
our Convention? Is not the politicization of the Southern
Baptist Convention a clear sign that the lordship of Jesus
Christ is not preeminent in our fellowship? Has it not
become clear that we are in danger of becoming more like
a State than the Body of Christ? Is it not apparent in our
Convention that political strategy is more significant than
the struggle for faithfulness to God's claim on us in Jesus
Christ?

Secondly, Barth might ask: "Is there not a danger that
you Southern Baptists as a dominant denomination in
America may lose your identity as a 'church' because of an
uncritical affiance with American culture?" Is there not
something for us to learn from the tragedy of the German
Christian defection? Is our profession of the separation of
Church and State denied by a largely unconscious and

uncritical alliance with our nation as especially blessed of God? Do we assume uncritically that our nation is "under God"? How can we escape the charge that our church practices and attitudes, as well as our political choices, contributed significantly to racism in the South and in our nation? Has the passage of Civil Rights legislation or a deeper grasp of God's unqualified love for all without respect to race made us more sensitive to the rights and needs of minorities, the poor, and dispossessed? Are we able to see that God was working in and through the State to bring about equal rights for all persons under the law because it accorded with God's will that justice be done?

Finally, we would concur with Barth that it is right and just that as Baptist churches we have freedom to proclaim the gospel of God's reconciling love in Jesus Christ to all within the State. But with Barth we also need to ask how our churches, Convention, and we as believers should work toward a more just State sensitive to the weakest and most needy among us. Barth warns us that our political actions and decisions—our "political service" of God— must not be determined by rigid allegiance to political ideologies or programs. It is more important to act concretely in each new situation in response to God's all inclusive love for humanity revealed and actual in Jesus Christ. If we do this, we will act in the social and political arena in the attempt to make "human life more human" (Paul Lehmann). In so doing, our actions will serve God's coming kingdom and his perfect will.

ENDNOTES

1 George Hunsinger, ed., *Karl Barth and Radical Politics* (Philadelphia: Westminster, 1976), p. 181.

2 *Ibid.*, pp. 181–82.

3 *Ibid.*, p. 182.

4 *Ibid.*, pp. 181–83.

5 *Ibid.*, pp. 181–84.

6 *Ibid.*, p. 184.

7 Marquardt's book, *Theologie und Sozialismus: Das Beispiel Karl Barths* (1972) is not to my knowledge translated into English. He summarizes his thesis in "Socialism in the Theology of Karl Barth," in George Hunsinger, op. cit., pp. 47–76. Hunsinger includes essays responding to Marquardt.

8 Karl Barth, *The Word of God and the Word of Man*, tr. Douglas Horton (New York: Harper, 1957), p. 100.

9 See this programmatic statement included in Hunsinger, op. cit., pp. 19–45. Information on this period in Barth's career is available in the invaluable study of Eberhard Busch, *Karl Barth*, tr. John Bowden (Philadelphia: Fortress, 1976), pp. 60–125.

10 Karl Barth and Eduard Thurneysen, *Revolutionary Theology in the Making: Barth-Thurneysen Correspondence, 1914–1925*, in James D. Smart (Richmond: John Knox, 1964), p. 28. Other Barth writings relating to his socialism can be found in *The Beginnings of Dialectic Theology*, ed. by James M. Robinson (Richmond: John Knox, 1968). See also my *Karl Barth* (Waco: Word, 1972), ch. 1, for an overview of Barth's life and thought. Elizabeth B. Barnes develops the relevance of the "radical" Barth's emphasis on the church's social and political action in the world as a model for enriching a Southern Baptist ecclesiology. See *An Afront to the Gospel? The Radical Barth and the Southern Baptist Convention* (Atlanta: Scholars Press, 1987).

11 Some attention to Barth's dialectical theology can be found in my Karl *Barth*, pp. 21–30. In *my Foundation of Karl Barth's Doctrine of Reconciliation: Jesus Christ Crucified and Risen* (Lewiston: Edwin Mellen Press, 1991), I deal in ch, 1 with "The Early Barth and His Critics, 1919–1934."

12 Documentation for these emphases may be found in David L. Mueller, *Karl Barth*, pp. 30–93, 140–55; and in "The Contributions and Weaknesses of Karl Barth's View of the Bible," in *The Proceedings of the Conference on Biblical Inerrancy, 1987* (Nashville: Broadman, 1987), pp. 423–447. Also see *my* "Karl Barth and the Heritage of the Reformation," *Review and Expositor* (86, no, 1, 1989), pp. 45–64.

13 On the background and history of the German Church Struggle, see Arthur C. Cochrane, *The Church's Confession Under Hitler* (Philadelphia: Westminster, 1962); for the definitive treatment of the relationship of the Churches to the Nazi State, see Klaus Scholder, *The Churches and the Third Reich*, tr. John Bowden (Philadelphia: Fortress, 1988), 2 vols. It should be noted that the "Evangelical" Church in Germany refers to the dominant Protestant Lutheran Church as distinguished from the Protestant Reformed (Calvinistic/Presbyterian) and Catholic Churches. The term "Evangelical" is a derivative from the German word, *Evangelium*, which is closely linked to the word, "evangel," or "gospel." "Evangelical" is thus not to be confused with the customary English connotation of "Evangelical."

14 Karl Barth, *Theology and Church: Shorter* Writings 1920–1928, tr. Louise Pettibone Smith (New York: Harper, 1962), p. 133.

15 Cochrane, *op. cit.*, p. 74.

16 *Ibid.*, cited by Cochrane.

17 *Ibid., p.* 74. Cochrane includes the Guiding Principles of the "German Christians" in Appendix II, pp. 222–223.

18 Karl Barth, "Abschied von 'Zwischen den Zeiten,'" in *Anfänge der dialektischen Theologie*, ed. by Jurgen Moltmann (Munich: Chr. Kaiser Verlag München, 1963), Part II, pp. 313–318. My translation. Brackets inserted.

19 Cited in Cochrane, *op. cit.*, p. 41.

20 Cited in Cochrane, *op. cit.*, p. 40; brackets inserted.

21 Material in the following paragraph is cited from Cochrane, *op. cit.*, p. 222–23; cf. also pp. 74–180.

22 Cited in Cochrane, *op. cit.*, p. 222.

23 Busch, *Karl Barth*, p. 245.

24 Cited in Cochrane, *op. cit.*, pp. 222–23; bracketed material inserted.

25 Cited in Cochrane, op. cit., p. 239. For "The Barmen Declaration," see *Creeds of the Churches*, ed. by John H. Leith (Richmond: John Knox, 1973).

26 Cited in Cochrane, *op. cit.*, p. 241.

27 For an analysis of Barth's important publications and lectures in the thirties, see Busch, *op. cit.*, pp. 189–286.

28 See Karl Barth, *Eine Schweizer Stimme*, 1938–1945 (Zurich: Evangelischer Verlag, 1945). An abbreviated English version is *This Christian Cause* (New York: Macmillan, 1941). Other relevant publications include, *Trouble and Promise in the Struggle of the Church in Germany* (Oxford: Clarendon Press, 1938); *The Church and the Political Problem of Our* Day (London: Hodder and Stoughton, 1939); for post-war essays, see *Against the Stream: Shorter Post-War Writings, 1946–1952* (New York: Philosophical Library, 1954).

29 The reader is referred to Will Herberg's instructive essay, "The Social Philosophy of Karl Barth," which introduces the collection of

Barth's essays entitled, *Community, State and Church* (Garden City, New York: Doubleday, 1960).

30 My analysis follows the divisions of Barth's article. Citations are without page numbers, but within the sections indicated.

31 A recent collection of essays on Barth includes several on his "Ethics and Politics." See Nigel Biggar, ed., *Reckoning with Barth* (Oxford: Mowbray, 1988); cf. especially Rowan Williams, "Barth, War and the State," pp. 170–90. For bibliography on Barth's view of the State, see note 15, p. 213.

The title "Justification and Justice" indicates the question with which I am dealing in this work.

First of all, I will state the question thus: Is there a connection between the justification of the sinner through faith alone, completed once for all by God through Jesus Christ, and the problem of justice, the problem of human law? Is there an inward and vital connection by means of which in any sense human justice (or law), as well as divine justification, becomes a concern of Christian faith and Christian responsibility, and therefore also a matter which concerns the Christian Church? But we may clearly ask the same question with reference to other conceptions; take the problem of *order*, for instance, of that order which is no longer, or not yet, the Order of the Kingdom of God; or the problem of *peace*, which is no longer, or not yet, the eternal Peace of God; or the problem of *freedom*, which is no longer, or not yet, the freedom of the Children of God—do all these problems belong to the realm of the "new creation" of Man through the Word of God, do they all belong to his sanctification through the Spirit? Is there, in spite of all differences, an inner and vital connection between the service of God in Christian living indicated in James i. 27 and what we are accustomed to call "Divine Service" in the worship of the Church as such, and another form of service, what may be described as a "polit-

ical" service of God, a service of God which, in general
terms, would consist in the careful examination of all
those problems which are raised by the existence of human
justice, of law, or, rather, which would consist in the recognition, support, defence and extension of this law—and all
this, not in spite of but because of divine justification? In
what sense can we, may we and must we follow Zwingli,
who, in order to distinguish them and yet to unite them,
speaks in the same breath of "divine and human justice"?

It should be noted that the interest in this question
begins where the interest in the Reformation confessional
writings and Reformation theology as a whole ceases, or
rather, to put it more exactly, where it begins to fade (I).
The fact that both realities exist: divine justification and
human justice, the proclamation of Jesus Christ, faith in
Him and the office and authority of the secular power, the
mission of the Church and the mission of the State, the
hidden life of the Christian in God and also his duty as a
citizen—all this has been clearly and powerfully emphasized for us by the Reformers. And they also took great
pains to make it clear that the two are not in conflict, but
that they can very well exist side by side, each being com-
petent in its own sphere. But it must be strongly
emphasized that on this point they do not by any means
tell us all that we might have expected—not excepting
Luther in his work *Of Worldly Authority* of 1523 or Calvin
in the majestic closing chapters of his *Institutio*. Clearly we
need to know not only that the two are not in conflict,
but, first and foremost, to what extent they are connected.
To this question, the question as to the relationship
between that which they maintained *here* (with the great-
est polemical emphasis), and the *centre* of their Christian

message, we receive from the Reformers either no answer
at all, or, at the best, a very inadequate answer. Whatever
our attitude may be to the content of that last chapter of
the *Institutio, "De Politica Administratione"* (and, so far as
we are concerned, we are prepared to take a very positive
position), this at least is clear, that as we look back on the
earlier parts of the work, and in particular on the second
and third books and their cardinal statements about Jesus
Christ, the Holy Spirit, sin and grace, faith and repentance, we feel like a traveller, suddenly transported to a
distant land, who is looking back at the country from
which he started. For on the question of how far the *politica administratio* in the title of the fourth book belongs to
the *externis mediis vel aciminiculis quibus Deus in Christi
societatem nos invitat et in ea retinet* we shall find only the
most scattered instruction, for all the richness which the
book otherwise contains. But the same is true of the corresponding theses of Luther and Zwingli, and of those of the
Lutheran and Reformed Confessional writings. That
authority and law rest on a particular *ordinatio* of divine
providence, necessary on account of unconquered sin,
serving to protect humanity from the most concrete
expressions and consequences of that sin, and thus to be
accepted by humanity with gratitude and honour—these
are certainly true and biblical thoughts, but they are not
enough to make clear the relationship between this issue
and the other, which the Reformation held to be the decisive and final issue of faith and confession. What does
Calvin mean when, on the one hand, he assures us; "*spiri-
tuale Christi regnum et civilem ordinationem res esse
plurimum sepositas*" (2)— and on the other hand twice (3)
points to the subjection of all earthly rulers to *Christ*, indi-

cated in the passage, Psalms ii. I off., and describes the ideal outcome of that divine *ordinatio* as the *politia Christiana?* (4) How far *Christiana?* What has Christ to do with this matter? we ask, and we are left without any real answer, as though a particular ruling of a general, somewhat anonymous Providence were here the last word. And if we read Zwingli's strong statement, (5) that the secular power has "strength and assurance from the teaching and action of Christ," the disappointing explanation of this statement consists only in the fact that in Matthew xxii. 21 Christ ordained that we should render unto Caesar the things which are Caesar's and unto God the things which are God's, and that by paying the customary "tribute money" (*Didrachmon:* Matt. xvii. 24f.) he himself confirmed this teaching. That is again quite true in itself,[6] but, when stated thus apart from its context, in spite of the appeal to the text of the Gospel, it is based not on the Gospel but on the Law.

We can neither overlook nor take lightly this gap in the teaching that we have received from the fathers of our church—the lack of a gospel—foundation, that is to say, in the strictest sense, of a Christological foundation, for this part of their creed. There is, of course, no question that here too they only wished to expound the teaching of the Bible. But the question remains: in introducing these biblical data into their creed, were they regulating their teaching by the standard which elsewhere they considered final? That is, were they founding law on justice or justification? Political power on the power of Christ? Or were they not secretly building on another foundation, and, in so doing, in spite of all their apparent fidelity to the Bible, were they not actually either ignoring or misconstruing the fundamental truth of the Bible?

Let us consider what would happen if that were so: if the thought of human justice were merely clamped on to the truth of divine justification, instead of being vitally connected with it. On the one hand, to a certain extent it would be possible to purify the truth of divine justification from this foreign addition, and to build upon it a highly spiritual message and a very spiritual Church, which would claim to expect "everything from God," in a most devout spirit, and yet, in actual fact, would dispute this "everything" because, by their exclusive emphasis upon the Kingdom of God, forgiveness of sins and sanctification, they had ceased to seek or find any entrance into the sphere of these problems of human justice. On the other hand, it would be possible to consider the question of human law very seriously (still, perhaps, in relation to the general divine providence, but freed from the Reformers' juxtaposition of human justice and divine justification) and to construct a secular gospel of human law and a secular church, in which, in spite of emphatic references to "God," it would inevitably become clear that this Deity is not the Father of our Lord Jesus Christ, and that the human justice which is proclaimed is in no sense the justice of God. Since the Reformation it is evident that these two possibilities—and with them Pietistic sterility on one hand, and the sterility of the Enlightenment on the other—have been realized in many spheres. But it cannot be denied that there is a connection between this fact and that gap in the Reformers' teaching.

And now we live today at a time when, in the realm of the Church the question of divine justification, and in the realm of the State (lit.: political life), the question of human law, are being raised with new emphasis, and we seem, now as then, to be pressing onward towards developments that cannot yet be foreseen. It is obvious to recall that both justification and justice, or the Kingdom of Christ and the kingdoms of this world, or the Church and the State, formerly stood side by side in the Reformation confession, and that by "worship in spirit and in truth" the Reformers understood a life in both these realms. But if we are not once more to drift into sterile and dangerous separations, it will not be enough to recollect the Reformation, to repeat the formulae in which it placed the two realms side by side, to recite over and again (with more or less historical accuracy and sympathetic feeling) "the Reformed conception of the State" and the like, as though that gap were not evident, as though the Reformation teaching did not, with that gap, bear within itself the temptation to those separations. If the intensity of our present situation is to be our salvation and not our ruin, then the question which we asked at the outset must be put: Is there an actual, and therefore inward and vital, connection between the two realms?

What is offered here is a study—a biblical, or more exactly, a New Testament study—for the answer to this question. For the dubious character of the Reformation solution is decidedly due to the questionable character of the authoritative scriptural arguments on this subject presented at that time. If we are to progress further today, we must at all costs go back to the Scriptures. This pamphlet represents a partial attempt in this direction.[7]

I shall begin by reproducing in a few sentences what is, as far as I can see, the latest important statement of theological thought upon this subject: the work presented on our theme by K. L. Schmidt in his Basle inaugural lecture of December 2, 1936, under the title, "The Conflict of Church and State in the New Testament Community."[8] The fundamental teaching of the Church on her relation to the State is "the harsh picture of the execution of Jesus Christ by the officials of the State." What is this State? It is one of those angelic powers (ἐξουσίαι) of this age, which is always threatened by "demonization," that is, by the temptation of making itself an absolute. And, over against this State, what is the Church? It is the actual community (πολίτευμα) of the new Heaven and the new Earth, as such here and now certainly still hidden, and therefore in the realm of the State a foreign community (ποροικία). But the solidarity of distress and death unites Christians with all men, and so also with those who wield political power. Even though the Church prefers to suffer persecution at the hands of the State, which has become a "beast out of the pit of the abyss," rather than take part in the deification of Caesar, yet it still knows that it is responsible for the State and for Caesar, and it finally manifests this responsibility, "the prophetic service of the Church as Watchman," in its highest form by praying for the State and for its officials in all circumstances.

Schmidt's presentation is explicitly confined to one section only of the problem of the "Church and State in the New Testament," namely, with the question that appears to be directly opposed to ours: the question of the *conflict* between the two realms. But it seems to me important to determine that even in this other aspect of the problem, investigation of the New Testament inevitably reveals a whole series of view-points which are of the high-

est importance for the answer to our question about the
positive connection between the two realms. This is so
clear, that in what follows I shall confine myself simply to
the order traced by Schmidt.

I

THE CHURCH AND STATE AS THEY CONFRONT ONE ANOTHER

I too consider it right and important to point first of all to the situation in which *Jesus and Pilate* confront one another. So far as I can see, the Reformation writers in their teaching about Church and State, among all the somewhat significant Gospel texts that are concerned with this encounter, were interested only in the words of John xviii. 36: "My Kingdom is not of this world." Their thoughts about the Electoral Prince of Saxony or the Council of Zürich or Geneva would clearly have been disturbed, had they concentrated intensively upon the person of Pilate. But did the Reformers see clearly at this point? Is a "disturbance" all that can be expected? Might they not perhaps have found here a better foundation for what they wished to say on this matter? Here, at any rate, we must try to fill up the gap which they have left.[9]

In point of fact, in this encounter two points stand out with an almost blinding clarity: the State, in its "demonic" form, and thus its authority as the "power of the present age," on the one hand; the homelessness of the Church in this age, on the other hand. If the "rulers[10] of this world" had recognized the wisdom of God, which "we," the apostles, speak to the perfect, then "they would not have crucified the Lord of Glory" (I Cor. ii. 6f.). There they showed that they did not recognize the wisdom of God. But the teaching on the separation between Church and State was not, and is not, the only teaching which the Church may glean from the passages concerned with the encounter between Jesus and Pilate.

I turn next to John xix. 11; here Jesus expressly confirms Pilate's claim to have "power" over Him, and not, indeed, an accidental or presumptuous power, but one given to him "from above."[11] And this power is in no sense in itself, and as such, a power of the Evil One, of enmity to Jesus and His claims. Pilate himself formulated the matter thus in the previous verse[10]: "I have power to release thee and power to crucify thee." As power given by God, it could be used either way towards Jesus without losing its divine character. Certainly, had Jesus been released by Pilate, that would not have meant that the claim of Jesus to be King would have been recognized. Who for this end was born, and for this end came into the world, that He should bear witness to the truth (John xviii. 37). Such "recognition" cannot be and is not Pilate's business. To the question of truth, the State is neutral. "What is truth?" But the release of Jesus, and with it the recognition by the "rulers of this world" of the wisdom of God, might have meant the possibility of proclaiming openly the claim of Jesus to be such a king; or, in other words, it would have meant the legal granting of the right to preach justification! Now Pilate did *not* release Jesus. He used his power to crucify Jesus. Yet Jesus expressly acknowledged that even so his power was given him by God. Did He thereby, in the mind of the evangelist, subject Himself to the will and the verdict of a general divine providence? Or does the evangelist mean that in the use Pilate made of his power, instead of giving a just judgment, actually, under the cloak of legality, he allowed injustice to run its course? Was the one thing, or at least the chief thing, he wanted to emphasize here: that the State, by this decision, turned against the Church?

No; what he means is that what actually took place in this use of the statesman's power was the only possible thing that could take place in the fulfillment of the gracious will of the Father of Jesus Christ! Even at the moment when Pilate (still in the garb of justice! and in the exercise of the power given him by God) allowed injustice to run its course, he was the human created instrument of that justification of sinful man that was completed once for all time through that very crucifixion.

Consider the obvious significance of the whole process in the light of the Pauline message: when Pilate takes Jesus from the hands of the Jews in order to have Him scourged and crucified, he is, so to say, the middleman who takes Him over in the name of paganism, who in so doing declares the solidarity of paganism with the sin of Israel, but in so doing also enters into the inheritance of the promise made to Israel. What would be the worth of all the legal protection which the State could and should have granted the Church at that moment, compared with this act in which, humanly speaking, the Roman governor became the virtual founder of the Church? Was not this claim confirmed, for example, in the testimony of the centurion at the Cross (Mk. xv. 39) which anticipates all the creeds of Christendom? Then there is another truth which the Church might *also* gather from the meeting of Jesus and Pilate: namely, the very State which is "demonic" may will evil, and yet, in an outstanding way, may be constrained to do good. The State, even in this "demonic" form, cannot help rendering the service it is meant to render. It can no more evade it in the incident recorded by Luke xiii. 1-5, where the same Pilate, the murderer of young Galileans, becomes at the same time the instrument of the call to repentance, in the same way as the—equally murderous—Tower of Siloam. This is why the State cannot lose the honour that is its due. For that very reason the New Testament ordains that in all circumstances honour must be shown to its representatives (Rom. xiii. 1-8; 1 Pet. ii. 17).

The synoptic accounts of the Barabbas-episode point in the same direction. What is Pilate doing when he releases the "notable" Barabbas, cast into "prison for insurrection and murder," but delivers "to scourging and crucifixion" the Jesus whom he has himself declared to be guiltless? For all our amazement at such justice, we may not overlook the fact that in that very act of the political authority, not one of the earliest readers of the Gospels could think of anything other than that act of God, in which He "made Him to be sin for us, who knew no sin, that we might be made the righteousness of God in Him" (2 Cor. v. 21). What is this extremely unjust human judge doing at this point? In an eminent and direct way he is fulfilling the word of the supremely just Divine Judge. Where would the Church be if this released Barabbas were in the place of the guiltless Jesus? If, that is, there had been no "demonic" State?

Finally, there is one other point in the passages referring to Pilate which must not be overlooked: Jesus was *not* condemned as an enemy of the State, as the "King of the Jews"—although, according to Matthew xxvii. 11; Mark xv. 2 He acknowledged Himself to be a king.[12] Strictly speaking, Jesus was never condemned at all. All four evangelists vie with one another in contending that Pilate declared Him innocent, that he regarded Him as "a just man" (Matt. xxvii. 19-24; Mk. xv. 14; Lk. xxiii. 14, 15, 22; John Xviii. 38; X1X. 4, 6).[13] Here too the connection with justification now becomes clear: this same Pilate, constrained to become the instrument of the death of Jesus, ordained by God for the justification of sinful man—this same Pilate is also forced to confirm the presupposition of this event: to affirm expressly and openly the innocence of Christ, and—of course—it is in this very fact that he is fulfilling his specific function. "Pilate sought to release Him" (John xix. 12). For it is in this sentence of acquittal (which he did *not* pronounce), that his duty lies. If he had done so the State would have shown its *true* face. Had it really done so, then acquittal would have had to follow, and the State would have had to grant legal protection to the Church! The fact that this did not actually happen is clearly regarded by the Evangelists as a deviation from the line of duty on the part of Pilate, as a failure on the part of the State. Pilate "delivered" Jesus to crucifixion, because he wished to satisfy the people (Mk. xv. 15). The political charge against Jesus was for Pilate clearly groundless, but he "gave sentence that it should be as they required" (Luke xxiii. 24). "Take ye him and crucify him!"

(John xix. 6). This decision has nothing to do with the law of the State nor with the administration of justice. The Jews themselves confirmed this: "*We* have a law and by *our* law he ought to die" (John xix. 7). It was not in accordance with the law of the State, but *in spite* of this law, and in accordance with a totally *different* law, and in flagrant defiance of justice, that Jesus had to die. "YE, the Jews, have killed Jesus!" is the cry throughout the New Testament, with the exception of I Cor. ii. 8 ; (Acts ii. 23; iii, 15; vii. 52; I Thess. ii. 15). In this encounter of Pilate and Jesus the "demonic" State does not assert itself too much but too little; it is a State which at the decisive moment fails to be true to itself. Is the State here an absolute? If only Pilate had taken himself absolutely seriously as a representative of the State he would have made a different use of his power. Yet the fact that he used it as he did could not alter the fact that this power was really given him "from above." But he could not use it as he did without contradicting his true function; under the cloak of legality he trampled on the law which he should have upheld; in so doing, however, it became evident that if he had been true to his commission he would have had to decide otherwise. Certainly, in deflecting the course of justice he became the involuntary agent and herald of divine justification, yet at the same time he makes it clear that real human justice, a real exposure of the true face of the State, would inevitably have meant the recognition of the right to proclaim divine justification, the Kingdom of Christ which is not of this world, freely and deliberately.

We must not again lose sight of this doubly positive determination of the encounter between these two realms, as it has emerged in this critical instance. Particularly in considering this most critical instance we cannot say that the legal administration of the State "has nothing to do with the order of Redemption"; that here we have been moving in the realm of the first and not of the second article of the Creed.[14] No, Pontius Pilate now belongs not only to the Creed, but to its second article in particular!

II

THE ESSENCE OF THE STATE

TURNING to the exegesis of the passage Romans xiii. 1-7, which has been so much studied in every age, it may be thought peculiar that although an ancient explanation mentioned by Irenaeus[15] was clearly not generally accepted, yet in recent years fresh emphasis has been laid[16] on the fact that the word ἐξουσίαι which is used by Paul in verse 1, and in Titus iii. 1 and also by Luke, to indicate political authority, is used throughout the rest of the New Testament, wherever it appears, in the plural (or in the singular with πᾶσα) (1 Cor. xv. 24; Col. i. 16; ii. 10, 15; Eph. i. 21; iii. 10; vi. 12; 1Pet. iii. 22) to indicate a group of those angelic powers which are so characteristic of the Biblical conception of the world and of man. ἐξουσίαι, like ἀρχαί or ἄρχοντες, δυνάμεις, θρόνοι, κυριότες, ἄγγελοι, etc., and all these entities which are so difficult to distinguish (probably they should all be included under the comprehensive heading ἄγγελοι) constitute created, but invisible, spiritual and heavenly powers, which exercise, in and above the rest of creation, a certain independence, and in this independence have a certain superior dignity, task, and function, and exert a certain real influence.

The researches of G. Dehn strengthen the already strong probability which arises from the language itself, that when the Church of the New Testament spoke of the State, the emperor or king, and of his representatives and their activities, it had in mind the picture of an "angelic power" of this kind, represented by this State and active within it. We have already met the concept ἐξουσία in the singular as indicating the power given to Pilate, to crucify Jesus or to release Him. Similarly, the concept ἄρχοντες (1 Cor. ii. 8) is certainly intended to designate the State—and an angelic power.[17] What does this mean? It has been rightly maintained[18] that this explains how it came to pass that the State, from being the defender of the law, established by God's will and ordinance, could become "the beast out of the abyss" of Revelation xiii.[19] dominated by the Dragon, demanding the worship of Caesar, making war on the Saints, blaspheming God, conquering the entire world. An angelic power may indeed become wild, degenerate, perverted, and so become a "demonic" power. That, clearly, had happened with the State as represented by Pilate which crucified Jesus. When Paul warns the Colossian Christians against the seductions of these angelic powers which have become "demonic," against a "worshipping of angels" (Col. ii. 18), when he exhorts them to strive not with flesh and blood but with principalities and powers, with "rulers of the darkness of this world" (Ephes. vi. 12), when he comforts them by the assurance that these "powers" cannot separate us from the love of Christ (Rom. viii. 38f.)[20], and when he gives the vision of their ultimate "deliverance" through Christ in

His Parousia (1 Cor. xv. 24)—all this may have a more or
less direct bearing upon the "demons" and the "demonic"
forces in the political sphere. But the last passage which
was quoted also contains a warning. When the separation
between Christ and the State has been established, the last
word on the vision of the "beast out of the abyss" has not
been said. I think it is dangerous to translate the word
καταργεῖν in 1 Corinthians xv. 24 as "annihilate"—however clearly it bears that meaning in other passages. For
immediately afterwards, in verse 25, the passage runs: "He
must reign till He hath put all His enemies under His
feet"—that is, till He has sovereign power over them. But
that is also the image used in Philippians ii. 9f.—
"Wherefore God also hath highly exalted Him, and given
Him a name which is above every name; that at the name
of Jesus every knee should bow, of things in Heaven and
things in earth and things under the earth"; in Ephesians i.
20, 21—"He set Him at His own right hand in the heavenly places far above all principality and power and
might..."; in 1 Peter iii. 22—"Who is gone into heaven
and is on the right hand of God; angels and authorities
and powers being made subject unto Him." The same
image, too, is used in that particularly striking passage:
Colossians ii. 15: "Having spoiled principalities and
powers, He made a show of them openly, triumphing over
them in it." The destiny of the rebellious angelic powers
which is made clear in Christ's resurrection and parousia is
not that they will be annihilated, but that they will be
forced into the service and the glorification of Christ, and
through Him, of God. And both the beginning and the
middle of their story also correspond to this ultimate destiny. I fail to see how one can say[21] without further ado

that they simply represent "the world which lives on itself
and by itself and as such is the antipodes and exact opposite of the creation": "In them the solitary world arises."
According to Colossians i. 15 it is rather the case that they
have been created in the Son of God as in the image of the
invisible God, by Him and unto Him, and further,
according to Col. ii. 10, that in Him they have their Head.
From the first, then, they do not belong to themselves.
From the first they stand at the disposal of Jesus Christ. To
them too His work is relevant: "He was seen of angels" (1
Tim. iii. 16). The outcome of St. Paul's preaching to the
heathen is that through the existence of the Church, the
"manifold wisdom of God"[22] might be made known unto
them (Eph. iii. 10). With the Church they too desire to
gaze into the mystery of the salvation which is to be
revealed in the future (I Pet. i. 12). And they are present
not only as spectators; for them too the peace won by the
crucifixion of Christ (Col. i. 20) and the ἀνακε-
φαλαίωσις (Eph. i. 10) are in both passages related both
to earth and to heaven. We should note that here there is
no question of any justification of the "demons" and the
"demonic" forces; nor is the function of Christ concerning
the angelic powers directly connected with divine justification. But it seems to have some connection with human
justice. For what seems to be meant here is that in Christ
the angelic powers are called to order and, so far as they
need it, they are restored to their original order. Therefore
any further rebellion in this realm can, in principle, only
take place in accordance with their creation, and within
Christ's order, in the form of unwilling service to the
Kingdom of Christ, until even that rebellion, within the
boundaries of the Kingdom of Christ, is broken down in

His Resurrection and Parousia. At the present time, in the period bounded by the Resurrection and the Parousia, there is no further rebellion of the heavenly powers ; no longer can they escape from their original order.

What follows when all this is applied to the political angelic power? Clearly this: that that power, the State as such, belongs originally and ultimately to Jesus Christ; that in its comparatively independent substance, in its dignity, it function and its purpose, it should serve the Person and the Work of Jesus Christ and therefore the justification of the sinner. The State can of course become "demonic," and the New Testament makes no attempt to conceal the fact that at all times the Church may, and actually does, have to deal with the "demonic" State. From this point of view the State becomes "demonic" not so much by an unwarrantable assumption of autonomy—as is often assumed—as by the *loss* of its legitimate, relative *independence*, as by a renunciation of its true substance, dignity, function and purpose, a renunciation which works out in Caesar—worship, the myth of the State and the like. We should add that, in the view of the New Testament, in no circumstances can this "demonic" State finally achieve what it desires; with gnashing of teeth it will have to serve where it wants to dominate; it will have to build where it wishes to destroy; it will have to testify to God's justice where it wishes to display the injustice of men.

On the other hand, it is not inevitable that the State should become a "demonic" force.[23] In the New Testament it is not suggested that by its very nature, as it were, the State will be compelled, sooner or later, to play the part of the Beast "out of the abyss." Why should this be inevitable, since it too has been created in Christ, through Him and for Him, and since even to it the manifold wisdom of God is proclaimed by the Church? It could not itself become a Church, but from its very origin, in its concrete encounter with Christ and His Church, it could administer justice and protect the law (in accordance with its substance, dignity, function and purpose, and in so doing remaining true to itself instead of losing itself!) In so doing, voluntarily or involuntarily, very indirectly yet none the less certainly, it would be granting the gospel of justification a free and assured course. In the light of the New Testament doctrine of angels it is impossible to ignore the fact that the State may also manifest its neutral attitude towards Truth, by rendering to the Church, as a true and just State, that service which lies in its power to render; by granting it its true and lawful freedom, that we may lead a quiet and peaceable life in all godliness and honesty" (I Tim. ii. 2). If, even when it has become an unjust State and a persecutor of the Church, it cannot escape the real subordination in which it exists, yet in the same real subordination it may also show its true face as a just State (in practice that may well mean at least a part of its true face) as, indeed, it appears to have manifested it to a great extent in all that concerns Paul, according to the Acts of the Apostles[24].

Thus there is clearly no cause for the Church to act as though it lived, in relation to the State, in a night in which all cats are grey. It is much more a question of continual decisions, and therefore of distinctions between one State and another, between the State of yesterday and the State of today. According to I Corinthians xii. 10 the Church receives, among other gifts, that of "discerning of spirits."

If by these "spirits" we are to understand the angelic powers, then they have a most significant political relevance in preaching, in teaching, and in pastoral work.

One decisive result of this exegesis as a whole should be a clear understanding of the meaning of Romans 13. The God from Whom all this concrete authority comes, by Whom all powers that be are ordained (v. 1), Whose ordinance every man resists who resists that power (v. 2), Whose διάκονος it is (v. 4) and Whose λειτουργοί its representatives are (v. 6)—this God cannot be understood apart from the Person and the Work of Christ; He cannot be understood in a general way as Creator and Ruler, as was done in the expositions of the Reformers, and also by the more recent expositors up to and including Dehn and Schlier. When the New Testament speaks of the State we are, fundamentally, in the *Christological* sphere; we are on a lower level than when it speaks of the Church, yet, in true accordance with its statements on the Church, we are in the same unique Christological sphere. It is not sufficient to state[25] that the ὑπὸ θεοῦ sweeps away all hypotheses which suggest that the origin of the State is in nature, in fate, in history, or in a social contract of some kind, or in the nature of society, and the like; this too is why it is not sufficient to state that the foundation of the State reminds it of its limits. The phrase ὑπὸ θεου does mean this, it is true, but it must be added that in thus stating this foundation and limitation of the State, Paul is not thinking of some general conception of God, in the air, so to speak, but he is indicating Him in Whom all the angelic powers have their foundation and their limits, the "image of the invisible God" Who as such is also "the first-born of all creation" (Col. i. 15). We need only see that for

Paul, within the compass of *this* centre and therefore *within* the Christological sphere (although outside the sphere characterized by the word "justification") there was embodied in the angelic world another secondary Christological sphere—if I may put it so—uniting the Church with the Cosmos, wherein the necessity and the reality of the establishment and administration of human justice was clearly important above all else—thus we need only see this in order to note that in Romans xiii. the Name of God is used in a very clear way, and not in any vague manner. The establishment and the function of the State, and, above all, the Christian's attitude towards it, will then lose a certain accidental character which was peculiar to the older form of exposition. We shall then not have to relate to God, as distinct from Jesus Christ, the grounds for the attitude required by i Peter ii. i, "for the Lord's sake"[26]; just as in the use of similar formulae in the epistles to the Colossians and the Ephesians, according to the specific witness of Colossians iii. 24 and Ephesians v. 20; vi. 6, no other "Lord" is meant than Jesus Christ. "Submitting yourselves one to another in the fear of Christ" (Eph. v. 21, R. V.). It is the fear of Christ—that is, the sense of indebtedness to Him as the Lord of all created lords (Col. iv. 1; Eph. vi. 9) which would be dishonoured by an attitude of hostility, and it is the fear of Christ which clearly, according to 1 Peter ii. i3f., forms the foundation for the imperative: "Submit yourselves...to the King." And we shall have to think in the same direction when in Romans xiii. 5 it is claimed of the same submission that it should occur not merely through anxiety before the wrath of authority, but for conscience' sake. Συνείδησις (conscience) means "to know with." *With whom* can man *know something?* The New Testament makes this quite clear. Schiatter has translated the συνείδησις θεοῦ of 1 Peter ii. 19 as "certainty of God." It is clear that in 1 Corinthians x. 25-27, where the formula used in Romans xiii. 5 also appears, it does not indicate a norm imposed upon mankind in general but one imposed on the Christian in particular—and that from the recognition of that norm implies that he must adopt a definite attitude. Christian knowledge, Christian certainty, and the Christian conscience do not demand that Christians should enquire in the shambles or at the feast about the origin of the meat that is set before them (1 Cor. x.). But the Christian conscience does demand that they should submit to authority (Rom. xiii.). Clearly this is because in this authority we are dealing indirectly, but in reality, with the authority of Jesus Christ.

III

THE SIGNIFICANCE OF THE STATE FOR THE CHURCH

In order to throw light upon the contrast between Church and State emphasis has always, rightly, been laid on the fact that the State (πολίτευμα) or the city (πόλις) of Christians should not be sought in the "present age" but in that "which is to come"; not on earth but in heaven. That is, in an impressive way, the theme of Philippians iii. 20; Hebrews xi. 10, 13-16; xii. 22; xiii. 14.And in Revelation xxi. this city of the Christians is surveyed and presented, with its walls, gates, streets and foundations: "The holy city, new Jerusalem, coming down from God out of heaven, prepared as a bride adorned for her husband" (v. 2). In this city there is, strikingly, no temple: "For the Lord God the Almighty, and the Lamb, are the temple thereof" (v. 22). That is why it is said: "The nations shall walk in the light of it: and the kings of the earth do bring their glory and honour into it. And the gates of it shall not be shut at all by day: (for there shall be no night there). And they shall bring the glory and honour of the nations into it. And there shall in no wise enter into it anything that

defileth, neither whatsoever worketh abomination or
maketh a lie; but they which are written in the Lamb's
book of life" (v. 24-27). It must here be emphasized, above
all else, that in this future city in which Christians have
their citizenship here and now (without yet being able to
inhabit it), we are concerned not with an ideal but with a
real State—yes, with the only real State; not with an imag-
inary one but with the only one that truly exists. And it is
the fact that Christians have their citizenship in this, the
real State, that makes them strangers and sojourners
within the State, or within the States of this age and this
world. Yes, if they are "strangers and pilgrims" here it is
because this city constitutes below their faith and their
hope—and not because they see the imperfections or even
the perversions of the states of this age and this world! It is
not resentment, but a positive sentiment, through which
in contradistinction to non-Christians it comes about, that
they have "no continuing city" here (Heb. xiii. 14). It is
because Paul knows that he is "garrisoned" by the Peace of
God which passes all understanding, that the *Pax Romana*
cannot impress Paul as an "ultimate."[27] It is because "the
saints shall judge the world" and not because the
Corinthian law-courts were particularly bad—that,
according to I Corinthians vi. 1-6, Christians must be
able, within certain limits, to renounce their right to
appeal to the law of the State and its courts of justice.

It is the hope of the new age, which is dawning in power,
that separates the Church from the State, that is, from the
States of this age and this world. The only question is
whether this same hope does not also in a peculiar way
unite the two. H. Schlier,[28] who rightly answers the ques-

tion in the affirmative, describes this bond as follows: "Whoever considers human life as ordered and established in faith, for this world which God is preparing…in face of the claims of the actual earthly bonds, and in the claims of the most exacting of all bonds—that of the State—will discern in them the will of God, and will see bonds established by God. In the eschatological knowledge about the actual end of the world, the present world is proclaimed in its real and true character as the creation of God's word." To that I would like to ask whether the New Testament anywhere shows any interest in the "present world in its real and true character as the creation of God" save in so far as it finds it to be grounded, constituted and restored in Christ? In this case, when we think of this bond, should we not do better to look forward, to the coming age, to Christ? rather than backward—that is, rather than think in the abstract about creation and the hypothetic divine bonds established by this creation.

Of one thing in the New Testament there can be no doubt: namely, that the description of the order of the new age is that of a *political* order. Think of the significant phrase: the Kingdom of God, or of Heaven, that it is called *Kingdom* of God or Heaven, and remember too the equally "political" title of the King of this realm: *Messias* and *Kyrios*. And from Revelation xxi. we learn that it is not the real church (ἐκκλησία) but the real city (πόλις) that truly constitutes the new age. Or, to put it otherwise, the Church sees its future and its hope, not in any heavenly image of its own existence, but in the real heavenly *State*. Wherever it believes in, and proclaims here and now, the justification of the sinner through the blood of the Lamb, it will see before it, "coming down out of Heaven from

God," the city of eternal *law* in which there is no offender and whose doors need never be closed, but which also needs no temple, for the same Lamb will be its temple. And this city will not endure merely on the ruins of the annihilated glory of the peoples and the kings of this earth, but the whole of this earthly glory will be brought into It, as supplementary tribute. Could the Church of divine justification hold the human law State in higher esteem than when it sees in that very State, in its heavenly reality, into which its terrestrial existence will finally be absorbed, the final predicate of its own grounds for hope? Deification of the State then becomes impossible, not because there is no divinity of the State, but because it is the divinity of the *heavenly* Jerusalem, and as such cannot belong to the *earthly* State. But the opposite of such deification, which would consist of making the State a devil, is also impossible. We have no right to do as Augustine liked to do, and straightway identify the *civitas terrena* with the *civitas Cain*. Not because its representatives, office-bearers and citizens can protect it from becoming the State of Cain, or even of the devil, but because the heavenly Jerusalem is also a State, and every State, even the worst and most perverse, possesses its imperishable destiny in the fact that it will one day contribute to the glory of the heavenly Jerusalem, and will inevitably bring its tribute thither.

From this point of view we can understand two passages from the Epistle to the Ephesians, in which the writer—although the word of the Kingdom of God which is not of this world was known to him, if not in those actual words, at least in reality—has no hesitation in describing the Church itself (in a connection in which he is considering its earthly and temporal reality) as the commonwealth of Israel (Eph. ii. 12) and later describes its members (in contradistinction to their past nature as strangers and foreigners) as fellow-citizens with the saints (Eph. ii. 19). There is no need to labour the point that this "politicizing" of the earthly Church is "from above," affirmed from the point of view of the ultimate reality, of the "last things," which, however, neither removes nor alters the fact that in this age, and in relation to the State, the Church is a "stranger." But, for that very reason, it is remarkable that the concepts, so important for the Christians, of "strangers and foreigners" are used to describe those who do not belong to the Church, and that the concept of the "rights of citizenship," so important for the ancient State, can become the predicate of the Church on earth. Here, too, we must ask whether the objection of the early Christians to the earthly State, and the consciousness of being "strangers" within this State, does not mean essentially that this State has been too little (and not too much!) of a State for those who know of the true State in heaven; or, again, we might put the question positively, and ask whether, in view of the basis and origin of the earthly State these Christians have not seen, in the Gospel of divine justification, the infinitely better, the true and only real source and norm of all human law, even in this "present age"? The desire or the counsel of Paul, in 1 Corinthians vi. 1-6, which so clearly points to something like legislation within the Church itself would otherwise be incomprehensible.

It is essential that we should arrive at this point—one might almost say at this prophecy: that it is the preaching of justification of the Kingdom of God, which founds, here and now, the true system of law, the true State. But it is equally essential that when this prophecy has been made the Church on earth should not go beyond its own bounds and endow itself with the predicates of the heavenly State, setting itself up in concrete fashion against the earthly State as the true State That it could and should do so cannot possibly be the meaning of Ephesians ii. and 1 Corinthians vi., because for the New Testament the heavenly State is and remains exclusively the *heavenly* State, established not by man but by God, which, as such, is not capable of realization in this age, not even in the Church. It was from the point of view of a later age that Clement of Alexandria[29] extolled the Church guided by the Logos as unconquered, enslaved by no arbitrary power, and even identical with the will of God on earth as in heaven; and again, later still, Augustine[30] was able to make the proud statement: "True justice is not to be found except in that republic, whose founder and ruler is Christ." It could be no accident that the writers of the Epistle to the Hebrews and the First Epistle of Peter neglected to console the Christians who were so homeless in this age and in this world by assuring them that nevertheless they had a home, here and now, in the Church. It is far more true that they have here no abiding city, and that the earthly Church stands over against the earthly State as a sojourning (παροικία) and not as a State within the State, or even as a State above the State, as was later claimed by the papal Church of Rome, and widened also by many a fanatical sect.

There are other conclusions to be drawn from Ephesians ii. and 1 Corinthians vi. This παροικία, this "establishment among strangers," does not wait for the city which is to come without doing anything. What indeed does take place in this παροικία? We might reply, simplifying, but not giving a wrong turn to the phrase: the preaching of justification. It is in this preaching that this "foreign community" affirms its hope in the city which is to come: in this preaching, that is, in the message which proclaims that by grace, and once for all, God has gathered up sinful man in the Person of Jesus, that He has made sin and death His own, and thus that He has not merely acquitted man, but that for time and for eternity He has set him free for the enjoyment of the life which he had lost. What the παροικία believes is simply the reality of this message, and what it hopes for is simply the unveiling of this reality, which still remains, here and now, concealed. We must note that it is not man or humanity, but the Lamb, the Messiah, Jesus, who is the Spouse for whom the Bride, the heavenly city, is adorned. It is He, and His Presence, as "the Lamb that hath been slain," who makes this City what it is, the City of Eternal Law. It is *His* law, the rights won by Jesus Christ in His death and proclaimed in His Resurrection, which constitute this Eternal law. (Here we are confronted by a quite different conception from the Stoic conception of the "City" to which Clement of Alexandria refers in the passage which we have mentioned.) Now this eternal law of Jesus Christ constitutes precisely the content of the message of justification, in which, here and now, the task of the Church consists. The Church cannot itself effect the disclosure of this eternal law, neither in its own members nor in the world. It cannot anticipate the "Marriage of the Lamb" (Rev. xix. 7). It cannot will to celebrate it in this "present age" but it can and it should proclaim it.

But—here we go a step further—it can and should
proclaim it to the world. It is worth noticing that in all
those passages in the Epistles that are directly concerned
with our problem a window is thrown open in this direction, which, at first sight, seems somewhat strange. The
behaviour towards the State which they demand from all
Christians is always connected with their behaviour
towards *all* men. "Render therefore to *all* their
dues....Owe *no man* anything but (which you can only do
within the Church) to love one another" (Rom. xiii. 7, 8).
In I Timothy ii. I we read that they should make "supplications, prayers, intercessions and giving of thanks for *all*
men," and in Titus iii. 2, immediately after the words on
those in authority, we read "be gentle, showing all meek-
ness unto *all* men." Finally in 1 Peter ii. 13 we are again
dealing with the *"Every* ordinance of man," and later in v.
17, going a step further (and here too in clear distinction
to the love of the brotherhood) "honour all men." What
does this mean? It seems to me, when considered in connection with I Timothy ii. 1-7, that it clearly means this:
Since it is our duty to pray for all men, so we should pray
in particular for kings and for all in authority, because it is
only on the condition that such men exist that we can
"lead a quiet and peaceable life in all godliness and honesty." Why is it necessary that we should be able to lead
such a life? Are we justified[31] in interpolating at this point
the words "as citizens," and so causing Christians to pray
for the preservation of a sort of bucolic existence? The passage quite clearly goes on to say: "for this (obviously the
possibility of our quiet and peaceable life) is good and
acceptable in the sight of God our Saviour, who will have
all men to be saved, and to come unto the knowledge of

the truth. For there is *one* God, and *one* mediator between God and men, the man Christ Jesus; who gave Himself a ransom for *all*, to be testified in due time. Whereunto I am ordained a preacher and an apostle." Thus the quiet and peaceable life under the rule of the State, for the sake of which this passage calls us to pray for statesmen, is no ideal in itself, just as the existence of the Church, in contradistinction to all other men, can be no ideal in itself. It is the preacher and apostle who stands in need of this quiet and peaceable life, and this apostle, and with him stand those with whom he here identifies himself, not in the service of a Universal Creator and Preserver, but in the service of the Saviour, God, who will "have all men to be saved and to come unto the knowledge of the truth," who is the one God in the one Mediator, who gave Himself a ransom for all. Why does the community need "a quiet and peaceable life"? It needs it because in its own way, and in its own place, it likewise needs the preacher and apostle for all, and because it needs freedom in the realm of all men in order to exercise its function towards all men. But this freedom can only be guaranteed to it through the existence of the earthly State which ordains that all men shall live together in concord, Is not the argument for submission to the civil administration of justice given in 1 Peter ii.15f., by the statement that it is the will of God that the Christians as those who are recognized by law as welldoers, "may put to silence the ignorance of foolish men—as free and not using their liberty" guaranteed by the State "for a cloak of maliciousness," but will act in this freedom as servants of God? Since this freedom of the Church can only be guaranteed through the existence of the State, therefore there is no alternative but that the Church should on its

side guarantee the existence of the State through its
prayers. That this mutual guarantee can and should fundamentally only be temporary—that is, that by its very
nature it can and should only be exercised in this age and
in this world, that the State can and should only partially
grant or totally deny the guarantee that the Church
demands of it, that, finally, the Church cannot and should
not require of the State any guarantee as to the validity or
the effectiveness of its gospel—all this is not the least
altered by the fact that the Church in all earnestness
expects this *limited* guarantee from the State, nor by the
fact that this guarantee which the Church requires of the
State is a serious one, and, as such, cannot be too seriously
laid upon the hearts of its members. Prayer for the bearers
of State authority belongs to the very essence of its own
existence. It would not be a Church if it were to ignore
this apostolic exhortation. It would then have forgotten
that it has to proclaim this promised justification to *all*
men.

But we must also understand the demand for loyalty
to the State in the other passages in the Epistles which deal
with this subject in the light of 1 Timothy ii., that is, in
the light of this mutual guarantee. In Titus iii. 1-8, aston-
ishingly enough, it is connected with the rebirth through
baptism and the Holy Spirit. But that is not astonishing if
the future heirs of eternal life, justified, according to v. 7
by the grace of Jesus Christ, receive all that not for themselves, but in the Church and as members of the Church
for all men, and thus stand in need of freedom not for
themselves but for the word of the Church and therefore
for human law, and so have to respect the bearers and representatives of that law. And when in Romans xiii. 3-4,

and 1 Peter ii 14 we read that obedience must be rendered to authority because it is the duty of authority to reward the good and to punish the evil, then in the context of both epistles it seems to me an impossible interpretation to say that the writers were speaking of "good" and "evil" in a quite general and neutral sense, and that the justice of the State is equally general and neutral. Why should not the writers have been making the same use of these concepts as they did elsewhere, and been demanding that Christians should do the good work of their faith, in the performance of which they, in contradistinction to the evil doers, have in no sense to fear the power of the State, but rather to expect its praise? Why, thinking of the "power" that was so clearly granted to Pilate to crucify or release Jesus, should they not first of all have pointed Christians to the better—i.e. the only true—possibility of the State, the possibility granted to it by the "good," i.e. by the Church, to protect the law (or, in other words, the possibility of a "Concordat"!)? The fact that the State could actually make use of the other possibility, that it could actually honour the evil and punish the good, may be quite true, but it cannot alter its mission, hence it does not affect the Christian attitude towards the State. Should the State go so far as to honour evil doers and to punish the good, if it can be recalled at all to its mission, and thereby to its own true possibility, it will be due to the Christian attitude towards it. And even if the State betrays its divine calling it will nevertheless be constrained to fulfill its function, to guarantee the freedom of the Church, even if in a quite different way! The "honour" that the State owes to the Church will then consist in the suffering of the followers of Christ, described in the First Epistle of Peter:—and the punishment of the evil doers will then consist in the fact that the glory of this suffering will be withheld from them. Thus in one way or another, the State will have to be the servant of divine justification.

Thus it is clear that in this very close relation between the existence of the Church and that of the State, the Church cannot itself become a State, and the State, on the other hand, cannot become a Church. It is true, of course, that in principle the Church, too, turns to all men; but it does so with its message of justification, and its summons to faith. The Church gathers its members through free individual decisions, behind which stands the quite different free choice of God, and in this age it will never have to reckon with gathering all men within itself. The Church must have complete confidence in God, who is the God of *all* men, and must leave all to Him. But the State has always assembled within itself all men living within its boundaries, and it holds them together, as such, through its order, which is established and maintained by force. The State as State knows nothing of the Spirit, nothing of love, nothing of forgiveness. The State bears the sword, and at the best, as seen in Romans xiii., it does not wield it in vain. It too must leave to God the question of what must be done for man's welfare in addition to the administration of the law which is based on force. The State would be denying its own existence if it wished to become a Church. And the Church on its side, for its own sake, or rather, for the sake of its mission, can never wish that the State should cease to be the State. For it can never become a true Church. If it were insane enough to attempt this it could only become an idolatrous Church. And, on the other hand, the Church would be denying its own existence if it wished to become a State, and to establish law by force, when it should be preaching justification. It could not be a true State; it could only be a clerical State, with a bad conscience on account of its neglected duty, and incapable, on this foreign soil, of administering justice to all men, as is the duty of the State.

But this relation between the Church and the State does not exclude—but includes—the fact that the *problem* of the State, namely, the problem of *law*, is raised, and must be answered, within the sphere of the Church on Earth. Those phrases in Ephesians ii. are no mere rhetorical flourishes, but they are concretely related to the fact that there is and must be within the Church itself (and here its close relation to the State asserts itself) *something like* (I am here deliberately using an indefinite phrase) a commonwealth: with its offices and orders, divisions of labour and forms of community. This is known as *Ecclesiastical Law*. It is well known that Rudolf Sohm regarded the appearance of ecclesiastical law (which, according to him, took place only in the second century) as the great sin of the early Church. But the Christian Church of the first century, as pictured by Sohm, moved freely by the Spirit of God, hither and thither, never actually existed. Now there is *one* fundamental ecclesiastical principle which cannot be denied without at the same time denying the resurrection of Christ and in so doing the very heart of the entire New Testament: the authority of the apostolate. And from the start there arose from this one principle many others, in freedom indeed, but in the freedom of the Word of God, and in no other freedom. The words of Paul (1 Cor. xiv. 33) about the God who is the author not of confusion but of peace, and above all the

whole argument of i Corinthians xii.—xiv., are characteristic at this point. How could the Church expect law from
the State and at the same time exclude law from its own
life? How could it, and how can it, live out the teaching
with which it has been entrusted and yet, in its own realm,
dispense with law and order, with the order which serves
to protect that teaching? Certainly, in the primitive
Church there was not more than "something like a commonwealth"; it was certainly never a juridical community
employing the methods of compulsion characteristic of
the State; and when, later on, it became such a body it was
to its own undoing. Ecclesiastical authority is spiritual
authority—authority, that is, which implies the witness of
the Holy Spirit. Does this make it less strict? Is it not for
that very reason the strictest authority of all? Was there
ever a more compelling legal order than that which we
find presupposed in the letters of the Apostles?

But the other side of the question, in this connection,
is still more remarkable: this antagonistic relation between
Church and State does not exclude—on the contrary, it
includes —the fact that the New Testament, if we examine
it closely, in no sense deals with the order of the State, and
the respect that is due to such an order, as something
which only affects the life of the Christian community
from without, but *to a certain extent* (and again I am deliberately using an indefinite phrase), the New Testament
deals with it as the question of a kind of annexe and out-
post of the Christian community, erected in the world
outside, which thus, in a certain sense, is included within
the ecclesiastical order as such. The fact that the Church
has had to assume a "certain" political character is bal-
anced by the fact that the Church must recognize, and

honour, a "certain" ecclesiastical character in the State. At all times indeed forms of "State Church" have always existed, which, in this respect at least, were not so far removed from the New Testament picture of things as might appear at first glance. It should be noted that the exhortation on the subject of the State in Romans xiii. cannot possibly, if taken in its context, be regarded as an exceptional statement dealing with the Law of Nature, because it is firmly embedded in the midst of a series of instructions all of which have as their presupposition and their aim the Christian existence as such. In the First Epistle to Timothy it stands at the head of a series of exhortations dealing with the conduct of men and of women during worship, and with the office of the bishop and of the deacon. In the Epistle to Titus it stands at the end, and in the First Epistle of Peter at the beginning, of a similar series. The verb "be subject unto," so characteristic of the imperative of this exhortation (Rom. xiii. 1; Titus iii. 1; 1 Pet. ii. 13), is not only used in Titus ii. 9 and 1 Peter ii. 18 for the conduct of Christian slaves towards their masters, but also in Colossians iii. 18, Ephesians v. 22, Titus ii. 5, and 1 Peter iii. 1, 5 for the conduct of women towards men, in i Peter v. for the conduct of the younger towards the older members of the community, and in Ephesians v. 21 and 1 Peter v. 5 for the conduct of Christians towards one another within the Church.

How do the "higher powers," the "rulers," the king and his governors come into this society? Does not the fact that they are within this society clearly show that this is a specifically *Christian* exhortation, that the secular authority and our attitude to it are to some extent included in those "orders" in which Christians have to prove their obe-

dience to God? and indeed to the God who is revealed in
Jesus Christ? And what shall we say to the fact that the
State ruler in Romans xiii. 4 is characterized as the minister of God, and the State officials in Romans xiii. 6 with
their various demands on the public, as God's ministers?[32]
How do they come to receive this sacred name? It seems to
me clear that they do "to a certain extent" actually stand
within the sacred order, not—as was later said, with far
too great a servility—as *membra præcipua*, but as *ministri
extraordinarii ecclesiæ?*

The light which falls from the heavenly polis upon the
earthly *ecclesia* is reflected in the light which illuminates
the earthly *polis* from the earthly *ecclesia*, through their
mutual relation. If the question of how this mutual relation can be explained is not actually answered by 1
Timothy ii. coupled with Revelation xxi., then a better
explanation would have to be found. But in any case, as
such, the phenomenon cannot well be denied.

IV

THE SERVICE WHICH THE
CHURCH OWES THE STATE

If we review the New Testament exhortations to Christians on the subject of their relation to the State, we are certainly justified in placing intercession (1 Tim. ii.) in a central position, as being the most intimate of all, and the one which includes all others. But we must be careful to see just how all-inclusive this particular exhortation is. Christians are called to offer "supplications, prayers, intercessions and thanksgivings" for all men, and in particular for kings and all who are in positions of authority. Does the passage actually say less than this: that the Church has (not as one incidental function among others, but in the whole essence of its existence as a Church) to offer itself to God for all men, and in particular for the bearers of State power? But this "offering oneself *for*" all men means (for that is the significance of the ὑπέρ) that the Church is fulfilling, on its side, that worship of God which men cannot and will not accomplish, yet which must be accomplished. This intercession is necessary because from God alone can rulers receive and maintain that power which is so salutary

for the Church, and, for the sake of the preaching of justification, so indispensable to all men. Far from being the
object of worship, the State and its representatives need
prayer *on their behalf.* In principle, and speaking compre-
hensively, this is the essential service which the Church
owes to the State. This service includes all others. In so
doing could the Church more clearly remind the State of
its limits? or more clearly remind itself of its own freedom?
than in thus offering itself on its behalf?

But this service must of course be rendered without
asking whether the corresponding service owed by the
State to the Church is also being given, and indeed without inquiring whether the individual bearers of State
power are worthy of it. How could such inquiry be made
before rendering a service of this kind? Clearly the service
becomes all the more necessary the more negative the
answer to the question; just as the nature of justification
comes out still more clearly when we see that he who is
"justified" is evidently a real and thorough sinner in the
sight of God and man. Thus the more negative the answer
to this question, the more urgently necessary is the priestly
duty laid upon the Church; the most brutally unjust State
cannot lessen the Church's responsibility for the State;
indeed, it can only increase it.

Our understanding of "Be in subjection..." in
Romans xiii. 1f. and the other passages, would have been
better served if we had not regarded this particular exhortation in the abstract, but had considered it in its
relationship to this first, primary exhortation. Can this
"subjection," fundamentally, mean anything other than
the practical behaviour on the part of the members of the
Church which corresponds to the priestly attitude of the

Church as such? "Be subject unto" (ὑποτασσεϲθαί) does not mean directly and absolutely "to be subject to someone," but to respect him as his office demands. We are here dealing with a subjection that is determined and conditioned by the framework within which it takes place, namely, by a definite τάξις (order). But the τάξις (as in other passages in which the word occurs) is not set up by the persons concerned who are to be the objects of respect, but, according to v. 2, it is based on the ordinance of God. It is on the basis, then, of this divine ordinance that such respect must be shown. But in what way can this due respect be shown to the leaders of the State, unless Christians behave towards it in the attitude of mind which always expects the best from it expects, that is, that it will grant legal protection to the free preaching of justification—but which is also prepared—under certain circumstances—to carry this preaching into practice by suffering injustice instead of receiving justice, and thereby acknowledging the State's power to be, in one way or another, God-given? If Christians were not to do this, if they were to oppose this ordinance and thus to refuse the State authority the respect which is determined and limited by divine decree, then, according to v. 2, they would be opposing the will of God, and their existence within the sphere of the State would become their condemnation. If they neither reckoned with this positive divine claim of the State nor were prepared if need be to suffer injustice at its hands, then by that very fact they would belong to those evil ones who must fear its power, and towards whom, by the use of its sword and the power of compulsion that is granted to it, it could only, openly or secretly ("power as such is evil") be the force which executes the

divine wrath, the dread manifestation of the perdition of
this age (vv. 4-5).

But this respect for the authority of the State which is
demanded in Romans xiii. must not be separated—in
theory or in practice—from the priestly function of the
Church. It cannot possibly consist of an attitude of
abstract and absolute elasticity towards the intentions and
undertakings of the State, simply because, according not
only to the Apocalypse, but also to Paul, the possibility
may arise that the power of the State, on its side, may
become guilty of opposition to the Lord of lords, to that
divine ordinance to which it owes its power. If Christians
are still to respect the State, even then, their docility in this
instance can only be passive, and, as such, limited. The
"subjection" can in no case mean that the Church and its
members will approve, and wish of their own free will to
further, the claims and undertakings of the State, if once
the State power is turned not to the protection but to the
suppression of the preaching of justification. Even then
Christians will never fail to grant that which is indispensable to the State power as guardian of the public law, as an
ordained power "tribute to whom tribute is due, custom to
whom custom, fear to whom fear, honour to whom (as
representative and bearer of ἐξουσία honour—even if the
State abuses this ἐξουσία, and demonstrates its opposition, as a demonic power, to the Lord of lords. Even then,
according to Matthew xxii. 21, Christians will render unto
Caesar the things which are Caesar's, i.e. whatever is his
due, not as a good or a bad Caesar, but simply as Caesar;
the right which is his, even if he turns that right to wrong.
As has been shown, it is and remains a God established
ἐξουσία, and that which we owe it, even then, must not

be withheld. But the fact also remains, unalterably, that Christians are to render unto God the things which are God's; and likewise, that the Church must be and must remain the *Church*. Thus the "subjection" required of Christians can *not* mean that they accept, and take upon themselves responsibility for those intentions and undertakings of the State which directly or indirectly are aimed against the freedom of preaching. Of course it must be understood that even then the "subjection" will not cease. But their submission, their *respect* for the power of the State to which they continue to give what they owe, will consist in becoming its victims, who, in their concrete action will not accept any responsibility, who cannot inwardly co-operate, and who *as* "subjects" will be unable to conceal the fact, and indeed ought to express it publicly, in order that the preaching of justification may be continued under all circumstances. All this will be done, not *against* the State, but as the Church's service *for* the State! Respect for the authority of the State is indeed an annexe to the priestly function of the Church towards the State. Christians would be neglecting the distinctive service which they can and must render to the State, were they to adopt an attitude of unquestioning assent to the will and action of the State which is directly or indirectly aimed at the suppression of the freedom of the Word of God. For the possibility of intercession for the State stands or falls with the freedom of God's Word. Christians would, in point of fact, become enemies of any State if, when the State threatens their freedom, they did *not* resist, or if they concealed their resistance—although this resistance would be very calm and dignified. Jesus would, in actual fact, have been an enemy of the State if He had *not* dared, quite

calmly, to call King Herod a "fox" (Luke xiii. 32). If the
State has perverted its God-given authority, it cannot be
honoured better than by this *criticism* which is due to it in
all circumstances. For this power that has been perverted
what greater service can we render than that of intercession? Who can render this service better than the
Christian? And how could Christians intercede, if, by
themselves acquiescing in the perversion of the power of
the State, they had become traitors to their own cause?
And where would be their respect for the State if it
involved such betrayal?

Through this discussion of the "subjection" of Romans
xiii. I (in its connection with I Timothy ii. I) we have
gained a fundamental insight into the nature of the service
which the Church, as the organ of divine justification,
owes to the State, as the organ of human law, which the
State has a right to expect from it, and by which, if it
remains obedient, it can actually assist the State. We have
affirmed that there is a mutual guarantee between the two
realms. We now ask: what is the guarantee which the
Church has to offer to the State?

After all that we have seen as constituting the relation
between the two realms, the answer must be given: that
apart from the Church, nowhere is there any fundamental
knowledge of the reasons which make the State legitimate
and necessary. For everywhere else, save in the Church, the
State, and every individual state, with its concern for
human justice, may be called in question. From the point
of view of the Church that preaches divine justification to
all men this is impossible. For in the view of the Church,
the authority of the State is included in the authority of
their Lord Jesus Christ. The Church lives in expectation of

the eternal State, and therefore honours the earthly State, and constantly expects the best from it: i.e., that, in its own way amongst "all men," it will serve the Lord whom the believers already love as their Saviour. For the sake of the freedom to preach justification the Church expects that the State will be a true State, and thus that it will create and administer justice. But the Church honours the State even when this expectation is not fulfilled. It is then defending the State against the State, and by rendering unto God the things that are God's, by obeying God rather than man, through its intercession it represents the only possibility of restoring the State and of saving it from ruin. States may rise and fall, political conceptions may change, politics as such may interest or may fail to interest men, but throughout all developments and all changes *one* factor remains, as the preservation and basis of all states— the Christian Church. What do statesmen and politicians themselves know of the authorization and the necessity of their function? Who or what can give them the assurance that this function of theirs is not, as such, an illusion, however seriously they may take it? And further, what do those others know, whose responsibility for the State and its law the statesman alone can represent, and on whose co-operation they are finally so dependent! Just as divine justification is the continuum of law, so the Church is the political continuum. And to be this is the Church's first and fundamental service to the State. The Church need only be truly "Church," and it will inevitably render this service. And the State receives this service, and secretly lives by it, whether it knows and gratefully acknowledges it or not, whether it wishes to receive it or not.

We only *seem* to be moving in a lower sphere when, turning again to Romans xiii., 5-7, we note that the Church here demands from her members, with an insistence elsewhere unparalleled, the fulfillment of those *duties* on the performance of which not merely the goodness or the badness of the State, but its very existence as a State depends. The fact that the right to impose rates and taxes belongs to the State, that its laws and their representatives should be honoured, as such, with all respect and reverence, can only be stated unreservedly and in a binding way from the standpoint of the divine justification of sinful man, because this provides the only protection against the sophisms and excuses of man, who is always so ready to justify himself and is always secretly trying to escape from true law. The Church knows that the State can neither establish nor protect true human law, "*ius unum et necessarium*," that is, the law of freedom for the preaching of justification, unless it receives its due from the Church, whereby alone it can exist as guarantor of law—that is why the Church demands that this due should be rendered in all circumstances.

We would of course give a great deal to receive more specific instruction in Romans xiii.—and elsewhere in the New Testament—about what is, and what is not to be understood by these particular political duties towards the State which are expected of the Church. The questions which arise in this connection cannot be answered directly from the New Testament; all that we can do is to give replies which are derived from the consideration of these passages by carrying the thought further along the same lines.

Could Romans xiii. 7, for instance, also mean: "an oath to whom an oath"? Does the rendering of an oath, if demanded by the State, belong to those duties that must be fulfilled? The Reformers, as we know, answered this question in the affirmative, but on looking at Matthew v. 33ff., we could wish that they had given a little more thought to the matter. So much, at least, is certain, even if the question is answered in the affirmative, that an oath to the State *cannot* be given (with true respect for the State!) if it is a "totalitarian" oath (that is, if it is rendered to a name which actually claims Divine functions). Such an oath would indeed imply that those who swear it place themselves at the disposition of a power which threatens the freedom of the Word of God; for Christians, therefore, this would mean the betrayal of the Church and of its Lord.

Again, is *military service* one of these self-evident duties to the State? The Reformers again answered this question in the affirmative, and again we could wish that they had done so with a little more reserve. Because the State "beareth the sword" (Rom. xiii.) it is clear that it participates in the murderous nature of the present age. Yet on this matter, at least in principle, we cannot come to a conclusion which differs from that of the Reformers. Human law needs the guarantee of human force. Man would not be a sinner in need of justification if it were otherwise. The State that is threatened from within or without by force needs to be prepared to meet force by force, if it is to continue to be a state. The Christian must have very real grounds for distrusting the State if he is to be entitled to refuse the State his service, and if the Church as such is to be entitled and called to say "No" at this point. A fundamental Christian "No" cannot be given here, because it would in fact be a fundamental "No" to the earthly State as such, which is impossible from the Christian point of view.

And here I should like to add, in relation to the question of national defence in Switzerland in particular, that here, too, there can for us be no practical refusal of military service. We may have grave misgivings about the way in which the Swiss State seeks to be a just state, but, all the same, we cannot maintain that it confronts the Church like "the Beast out of the abyss" of Revelation xiii. But this may and should be said of more than one other State today, against which it is worth while to defend our own legal administration. And since this is the case, from the Christian point of view we are right in seeking to defend our frontiers; and if the State in Switzerland takes steps to organize this security (it is not inconceivable that the Church should give its support to the State in this matter) we cannot close our eyes to the question of how far the Church in Switzerland should stand in all surety behind the State.[33]

It is quite another question whether the State has any right to try to strengthen its authority by making any kind of *inward* claim upon its subjects and its citizens; that is, whether it has any right to demand from them a particular philosophy of life (*Weltanschauung*), or at least sentiments and reactions dominated by a particular view imposed by the State from without. According to the New Testament, the only answer to this question is an unhesitating "No!" Claims of this kind can in no way be inferred from Romans xiii.; they have no legal justification whatsoever. On the contrary, here we are very near the menace of the

"Beast out of the abyss"; a just State will not require to make such claims. From Romans xiii.? It is quite clear that *love* is *not* one of the duties which we owe to the State. When the State begins to claim "love" it is in process of becoming a Church, the Church of a false God, and thus an unjust State. The just State requires, not love, but a simple, resolute, and responsible attitude on the part of its citizens. It is this attitude which the Church, based on justification, commends to its members.

Far more difficult, because far more fundamental, is another apparent gap in the teaching of the New Testament. It lies in the fact that the New Testament seems to speak concretely only of a purely authoritative State, and so to speak of Christians only as subjects, not as citizens who, in their own persons, bear some responsibility for the State. But it is to be hoped that the fulfillment of our political duty is not exhausted by the payment of taxes and other such passive forms of legality. For us the fulfillment of political duty means rather responsible choice of authority, responsible decision about the validity of laws, responsible care for heir maintenance, in a word, political struggle. If the Church were not to guarantee the modern State the fulfillment of such duties, what would it have to offer the "democratic" State? Here, too, we must ask: are we following a legitimate line of expansion of the thought of Romans xiii. ? It may seem audacious to answer that question in the affirmative, yet it must be firmly answered in the affirmative. Everything here depends on whether we are justified in this connection in taking the "be subject unto" of intercession in 1 Timothy ii. If the prayer of Christians for the State constitutes the norm of their "subjection," which would only be an "annexe" of the

priestly function of the Church, and if this prayer is taken
seriously as the responsible intercession of the Christians
for the State, then the scheme of purely passive subjection
which apparently—but only apparently—governs the
thought of Romans xiii., is broken. Then the serious question arises: is it an accident that in the course of time
"democratic" States have come into being, States, that is,
which are based upon the responsible activity of their citizens? [34]

Can serious prayer, in the long run, continue without
the corresponding work? Can we ask God for something
which we are not at the same moment determined and
prepared to bring about, so far as it lies within the bounds
of our possibility? Can we pray that the State shall preserve
us, and that it may continue to do so as a just State, or
that it will again become a just State, and not at the same
time pledge ourselves personally, both in thought and
action, in order that this may happen, without sharing the
earnest desire of the Scottish Confession[35]and saying, with
it: "*Vitæ bonorum adesse, tyrranidem opprimere, ab
infirmioribus vim improborum defendere,*" thus without, in
certain cases, like Zwingli[36] reckoning with the possibility
of revolution, the possibility, according to his strong
expression, that we may have to "overthrow with God"
those rulers who do not follow the lines laid down by
Christ? Can we give the State that respect which is its due
without making its business our own, with all the consequences that this implies? When I consider the deepest
and most central content of the New Testament exhortation, I should say that we are justified, from the point of
view of exegesis, in regarding the "democratic conception
of the State" as a justifiable expansion of the thought of

the New Testament. This does not mean that the separation between justification and justice, between Church
and State, the fact that Christians are "foreigners" in the
sphere of the State, has been abolished. On the contrary,
the resolute intention of the teaching of the New
Testament is brought out still more plainly when it is clear
that Christians must not only endure the earthly State, but
that they must *will* it, and that they cannot will it as a
"Pilate" State, but as a *just* State; when it is seen that there
is no outward escape from the political sphere; when it is
seen that Christians, while they remain within the Church
and are wholly committed to the future "city," are equally
committed to responsibility for the earthly "city," called to
work and (it may be) to struggle, as well as to pray, for it;
in short, when each one of them is responsible for the
character of the State as a *just State.* And the democratic
State might as well recognize that it can expect no truer or
more complete fulfillment of duty than that of the citizens
of the realm that is so foreign to it as a State—the Church
founded on divine justification.

There is one last point to be discussed concerning the
guarantee that the Church has to grant to the State. We
remember how the New Testament exhortation to a certain extent culminates in the affirmation that Christians
should render unto Caesar the things that are Caesar's by
their well-doing. But what does this mean if by this "well-
doing" we understand not a neutral moral goodness, but a
life lived in faith in Jesus Christ, the life of the Children of
God, the life of the Church as such? It then means that the
essential service of the Church to the State simply consists
in maintaining and occupying its own realm as Church. In
so doing it will secure, in the best possible way, the posi-

tion of the State, which is quite different. By proclaiming divine justification it will be rendering the best possible assistance to the establishment and maintenance of human justice and law. No direct action that the Church might take (acting partly or wholly politically, with well-meaning zeal) could even remotely be compared with the positive relevance of that action whereby, without any interference with the sphere of the State, this Church proclaims the coming Kingdom of Christ, and thereby the gospel of justification through faith alone; I mean that its action consists in true scriptural *preaching*, and *teaching*, and in the true and scriptural administration of the *sacraments*. When it performs this action the Church is, within the order of creation, the force which founds and maintains the State. If the State is wise, in the last resort it will expect and demand from the Church nothing other than this, for this includes everything that the Church can render to the State, even all the political obligations of its members. And we can and may formulate the matter even more precisely: the guarantee of the State by the Church is finally accomplished when the Church claims for itself the guarantee of the State, i.e. the guarantee of freedom to proclaim her message. This may sound strange, but this is the case: all that can be said from the standpoint of divine justification on the question (and the questions) of human law is summed up in this one statement: *the Church must have freedom to proclaim divine justification.* The State will realize its own potentialities, and thus will be a just State, in proportion as it not merely positively allows, but actively grants, this freedom to the Church; i.e., in proportion as it honourably and consistently desires to be the State within whose realm (whether as national Church or otherwise is a

secondary question) the Church exists which has this freedom as its right. We know that the earthly State is neither
called, nor able, to establish on earth the eternal law of the
heavenly Jerusalem, because no human beings are either
called, or able, to perform that task. But the State is called
to establish human law, and it has the capacity to do so.
We cannot measure what this law is by any Romantic or
Liberalistic idea of "natural law," but simply by the concrete law of freedom, which the Church must claim for its
Word, so far as it is the Word of God. This right of the
Church to liberty means the foundation, the maintenance,
the restoration of everything—certainly of all human law.
Wherever this right is recognized, and wherever a true
Church makes the right use of it (and the free preaching of
justification will see to it that things fall into their true
place) there we shall find a legitimate human authority
and an equally legitimate human independence; tyranny
on the one hand, and anarchy on the other, Fascism and
Bolshevism alike, will be dethroned; and the true order of
human affairs—the justice, wisdom and peace, equity and
care for human welfare which are necessary to that true
order, will arise. Not as heaven (not even as a miniature
heaven) on earth! No, this "true order" will only be able to
arise upon this *earth* and within the *present age*, but this
will take place *really* and *truly*, already upon this earth, and
in this present age, in this world of sin and sinners. No
eternal Solomon, free from temptation and without sin,
but none the less a Solomon, an image of Him whose
Kingdom will be a Kingdom of Peace without frontiers
and without end. This is what the Church has to offer to
the State when, on its side, it desires from the State nothing but freedom. What more could the State require, and

what could be of greater service to it than this—to be taken so inexorably seriously?

We all know the maxim of Frederick the Great: *Suum Cuique*. It is a less well-known fact that it already appears as a definition of human law, as a summary of the functions of the just State, in Calvin's *Institutio: at suum cuique salvum sit et incolume.*[37] But—this Calvin did not say, and this we must attempt to discover and to learn anew—it depends upon the justification of sinful man in Jesus Christ, and thus on the maintenance of this central message of the Christian Church, that all *this* should become true and valid in every sense, in the midst of this "world that passeth away," in the midst of the great, but temporary contrast between Church and State, in the period which the Divine patience has granted us between the resurrection of Jesus Christ and His return: Suum cuique.

ENDNOTES

1 Cf. the instructive composition of H. Obendiek: *Die Obrigkeit nach dem Bekenntnis der reformierten Kirche*, Münich, 1936.

2 *Inst.* IV., 20, 1.

3 *Ib.* 20, 5 and 29.

4 *Ib.* 20, 54.

5 *Schlussreden*, Art. 35.

6 Matt. xvii., dealing as it does with a Temple tax, does not really belong here.

7 The reader will do well to note that in this book one thing only is attempted: to move along the road of exegesis towards a better view of the problem "Church and State." It would in my opinion be a great advantage if some were to admit that such an attempt is necessary.

8 *Theologische Blätter*, 1937, No. 1. Since the completion of this work I have encountered Gerhard Rittel, *Das Urteil des neuen Testaments siber den Staat* (Zeitschr. f. Syst. Theol., 14. Jahrg. 1937, pp. 651–680, published in June 1938). It throws no new light on the subject with which I am concerned. On p. 665 of the essay we are asked to consider carefully "whether our exegesis is *true* exegesis, that is, whether its only goal is to discover what is given in the text or whether the writer's own wishes have—perhaps unconsciously—been introduced." Now, this is a warning that can always be heard to advantage. Only we are also entitled to ask for some restraint in their apostrophizing of others from those who cannot themselves be certain as to what they *must*, and what they *may not*, say on this subject. On p. 652, for example, the statements and the omissions on the subject of the "Fremdstaat" and the "Volksstaat" may well be as closely related to the "wishes" of the author as to those of certain "principalities and powers."

9 In the following passage I have found Calvin's views on the *sub Pontio Pilato of* the creed most illuminating. The passage is actually set in a quite different context.

Pourquoy n'est il dict simplement en un mot qu'il est mort, mais est parté de Ponce Pilate, soutsz lequel il a souffert?

Cela n'est pas seulement pour nous asseurer de la certitude de l'histoire: mais aussi pour signifier, que sa mort emporte condemnation.

Comment cela?

Il est mort, pour souffrir la peine qui nous estoit deue, et par ce moyen nous en delivrer. Or pource que nous estions coulpables devant le jugement de Dieu comme mal-faicteurs: pour representer nostre personne, il a voulu comparoistre devant le siege d'un iuge terrien, et estre condamn par la bouche d'iceluy: pour nous absoudre au throne du Juge celeste.

Neantmoins Pilate le prononce innocent et ainsi il ne le condamné pas, comme s'il en estoit digne (Matth. xxvii. 24; Luc. xxiii. 14).

Il y a l'un et l'autre. C'est qu'il est iustifié par le temoignage du iuge, pour monstrer, qu'il ne souffre point pour ses demerites, mais pour les nostres: et cependant est condamné solennellement par la sentence d'iceluy mesme, pour denoter, qu'il est vrayment nostre pleige, recevant la condamnation pour nous afin de nous en acquiter.

C'est bien dit. Car s'il estoit pecheur il ne seroit pas capable de souffrir la mort pour les autres: et neantmoins, afin que sa condamnation nous soit delivrance, il faut qu'il soit reputé entre les iniques (Jes. liii. 52).

Je l'entens ainsi.

(Catéchisme de l'Eglise de Genève, 1542. *Bekenntnisschriften der nach Gottes Wort reformierter Kirchen*, Münich, 1937f. Vol. I., p. 9.)

    10 "Archontes" is the title given in Rom. xiii. 3 to the officials of the State!

    11 In view of this passage, it seems to me impossible to say, as does Schlier (*Die Beurteilung des Staates im neuen Testament*, 1932, p. 312)*:* "The earthly State cannot possibly pronounce judgment on this Kingdom and its representatives." It was clearly called to do so

through the synagogue *of* the old Covenant (and, in the sense in which the Gospels use the words, it was certainly called to do so "non sine deo").

12 It is not correct to say that Jesus "fell a victim to a political charge." (G. Dehn, "Engel und Obrigkeit," *Theologische Aufsätze*, 1936, p. 91.)

13 I am indebted to Professor Ernst Wolf of Halle for the following: "On Ash Wednesday the Emperor kisses and gives gifts to the children of his orphanages; later in the procession, in the presence of the whole people, he enfeoffs or rather burdens the Minister of justice with the 'Inkwell of Pilate,' and as he lays it on the neck of the bowing man he says 'Judge with justice like him.' " A direct reminder of the scrupulously correct behaviour of Roman justice in matters pertaining to this mystery did not seem to the successors in the Imperium Romanum out of place in Holy Week; to Syrians and Abyssinians the "Landpfleger" and his spouse Procla were almost holy beings. ("Sir Galahad," Byzanz. *Von Kaisern, Engein und Eunuchen*, 1937, E. P. Tal and Co., Vienna, pp. 87–88.)

14 G. Dehn, op. cit., pp. 7 and 106.

15 Adv. o.h. V. 24, I.

16 Was H. Schlier ("Machte und Gewalten im neuen Testament," *Theologische Blätter*, 292) the first to express this? G. Dehn was in any case the first to develop the argument to any great extent.

17 And according to Rom. viii. 39 (οὔτε τις κτίσις ἑτέρα) we may not be far from the truth of the matter in describing the State as an ἀνθρωτίνη κτίσις (I Pet. ii. 13).

18 Cf. G. Dehn, op. cit., p. io8.

19 Cf. H. Schlier, "Vom Antichrist," *Theologische Aufsätze*, 1936, p. 11of.

20 I am surprised that G. Dehn (op. cit., p. 101) maintains the opposite point of view.

21 With H. Schlier, *Machte und Gewalten*, op. Cit., p. 291.

22 Probably Col. i. 26 may also belong here.

23 Political events of the last decades have introduced into New Testament exegesis on this matter a certain pessimism which seems to me not to be justified by the actual facts of the case. The State of Rev. xiii. is, as H. Schlier (*Die Beurteilung des Staates*, op. cit., p. 329) rightly maintains, "the borderline of the possible State."

24 Up to the present the κατέχον and κατέχων of 2 Thess. ii. 6ff. have been taken to indicate that function of the Roman State which works against the Antichrist. Had this interpretation not been "unfortunately" shattered by O. Cullmann, this passage would also have to be considered here. (*Le caractère eschatologique du devoir missionaire et de la conscience apostolique de St. Paul.* Recherches theologiques, Strasbourg, 1936, pp. 26–61.)

25 With H. Schlier, *Die Beurteilung des Staates*, op. cit., p. 323.

26 With G. Dehn, op. cit., p. 99.

27 Cf. K. L. Schmidt, op. cit., p. 8,

28 *Die Beurteilung des Staates*, op, cit., p. 320.

29 *Strom.* IV., 171, 2.

30 *Dc civ. Dei* II., 21.

31 With H. Schlier, *Die Beurteilung des Staates*, op. cit., p. 325.

32 In Rom. xv, 16 and Phil. ii. 25 Paul describes himself and his fellow-worker Epaphroditus as λειτουργὸν Ἰησοῦ χριστοῦ εἰς τὰ ἔθνη; in Heb. i. 2 the name is given to the angels of God and in Heb. viii. 2 to Christ Himself!

33 It is obvious that the same is also true of the Church in Czechoslovakia, in Holland, in Denmark, in Scandinavia, in France and, above all, in England.

34 Under this category it is proper to include also such "monarchies" as those of England and Holland. The assertion that all forms of government are equally compatible or incompatible with the Gospel is not only outworn but false. It is true that a man may go to hell in a democracy, and achieve salvation under a mobocracy or a dictatorship. But it is not true that a Christian can endorse, desire or seek after a mobocracy or a dictatorship as readily as a democracy.

35 Art. 14.

36 Schlussreden, Art. 42.

37 Inst. IV., 20, 3. And, as was kindly pointed out to me by Dr. Arnold Eberhard of Lörrach, there is no doubt that Calvin was on his side quoting Ulpian and Cicero.